Women and Property Rights in Indonesian Islamic Legal Contexts

Leiden Studies
in Islam and Society

Editors

Léon Buskens (*Leiden University*)
Petra M. Sijpesteijn (*Leiden University*)

Editorial Board

Maurits Berger (*Leiden University*) – R. Michael Feener
(*Oxford University*) – Nico Kaptein (*Leiden University*)
Jan Michiel Otto (*Leiden University*) – David S. Powers (*Cornell University*)

VOLUME 8

The titles published in this series are listed at *brill.com/lsis*

Women and Property Rights in Indonesian Islamic Legal Contexts

Edited by

John R. Bowen
Arskal Salim

BRILL

LEIDEN | BOSTON

Cover illustration: Village leader explains inheritance cases in Aceh, 2012.

Library of Congress Cataloging-in-Publication Data

Names: Bowen, John R. (John Richard), 1951-, editor. | Salim, Arskal, editor.
Title: Women and property rights in Indonesian Islamic legal contexts / Edited by
    John R. Bowen, Arskal Salim.
Description: Leiden : Brill, 2019. | Series: Leiden studies in Islam and society ; 8 |
    Includes bibliographical references and index.
Identifiers: LCCN 2018046673 (print) | LCCN 2018046868 (ebook) |
    ISBN 9789004386297 (E-book) | ISBN 9789004385962 (hardback : alk. paper)
Subjects: LCSH: Women–Legal status, laws, etc.–Indonesia. | Women (Islamic
    law)–Indonesia. | Right of property (Islamic law)–Indonesia.
Classification: LCC KNW517.5 (ebook) | LCC KNW517.5 .W66 2018 (print) |
    DDC 346.59804/32082–dc23
LC record available at https://lccn.loc.gov/2018046673

Typeface for the Latin, Greek, and Cyrillic scripts: "Brill". See and download: brill.com/brill-typeface.

ISSN 2210-8920
ISBN 978-90-04-38596-2 (hardback)
ISBN 978-90-04-38629-7 (e-book)

Copyright 2019 by Koninklijke Brill NV, Leiden, The Netherlands.
Koninklijke Brill NV incorporates the imprints Brill, Brill Hes & De Graaf, Brill Nijhoff, Brill Rodopi,
Brill Sense and Hotei Publishing.
All rights reserved. No part of this publication may be reproduced, translated, stored in a retrieval system,
or transmitted in any form or by any means, electronic, mechanical, photocopying, recording or otherwise,
without prior written permission from the publisher.
Authorization to photocopy items for internal or personal use is granted by Koninklijke Brill NV provided
that the appropriate fees are paid directly to The Copyright Clearance Center, 222 Rosewood Drive,
Suite 910, Danvers, MA 01923, USA. Fees are subject to change.

This book is printed on acid-free paper and produced in a sustainable manner.

Contents

Abbreviations   VII
Notes on Contributors   VIII
Note on Transliteration   XII

Introduction
Studying Women's Access to Property   1
　John R. Bowen and Arskal Salim

PART 1
Local Systems of Meaning, Norms and Power

1　The Social Practice of *Mahr* among Bimanese Muslims
　Modifying Rules, Negotiating Roles   15
　　Atun Wardatun

2　*Siri* and the Access of Bugis Makassarese Women to Property Rights　30
　　Rosmah Tami

PART 2
Women's Visions and Strategies

3　The Rights of Children Born out of Wedlock
　*Views of Muslim Women's Organizations on Constitutional Court
　Judgement 46/2010*　47
　　Tutik Hamidah

4　Inheritance for Women
　The Role of Lawyers in Women's Access and Rights　69
　　Nanda Amalia

PART 3
The Role of Judges

5 Women's Financial Rights after Divorce in Indonesia   89
   Euis Nurlaelawati

6 *Mut'ah* and *Iddah*
   Post-divorce Payment Practices in Aceh   107
   Abidin Nurdin

7 Disputing Marriage Payments in Indonesia
   A Comparative Study of Aceh and South Sulawesi   127
   Arskal Salim

   Epilogue   146
   John R. Bowen

   Glossary   155
   Index   158

Abbreviations

KHI	*Kompilasi Hukum Islam – Compilation of Islamic Laws*
Komnas Perempuan	*Komisi Nasional Anti-Kekerasan Perempuan* –National Commission on Violence Against Women
KPAI	*Komisi Perlindungan Anak Indonesia* – The Indonesian Commission for the Protection of Children
KUA	*Kantor Urusan Agama* – Religious Affairs Office
LAZ	*Lembaga Amil Zakat* – Non-government-sponsored zakat agency
LBH	*Lembaga Bantuan Hukum* – Legal Aid Institute
LBH APIK	*Lembaga Bantuan Hukum Asosiasi Perempuan* – Women's Association for Justice and Legal Aid
MPR	*Majelis Permusyawaratan Rakyat* – People's Consultative Assembly
MPU	*Majelis Permusyawaratan Ulama* – Ulama Consultative Council
MUI	*Majelis Ulama Indonesia* – Indonesian Council of Ulama
NU	*Nahdlatul Ulama* – Traditionalist Muslim mass organization
PBB	*Partai Bulan Bintang* – Moon and Crescent Party
PBNU	*Pengurus Besar Nahdlatul Ulama* – Nahdlatul Ulama Executive Board
PKI	*Partai Komunis Indonesia* – Indonesian Communist Party
PN	*Pengadilan Negeri* – District Court
PPP	*Partai Persatuan Pembangunan* – United Development Party
PTA	*Pengadilan Tinggi Agama* – Religious High Court
RT	*Rukun Tetangga* – Neighbourhood Governance Unit
RW	*Rukun Warga* – Community Governance Unit
SAW	*Salla Allah alaihi wa sallam* – PBUH (may Allah's peace and blessings be upon him)
SMA	*Sekolah Menengah Atas* – Senior High school
UIN	*Universitas Islam Negeri* – State Islamic University
UUD '45	*Undang-Undang Dasar Republik Indonesia* 1945 – Indonesian Constitution of 1945

Notes on Contributors

Nanda Amalia

is Lecturer at the Faculty of Law, University of Malikussaleh, Lhokseumawe Aceh – Indonesia. She received her Masters degree in law from Brawijaya University, Malang, East Java – Indonesia. From 2015, she is Vice Dean of the Faculty of Law. Nanda developed an interest in studying and researching on women's protection, women's participation in societies, and the legal awareness of the society. Some of her publications are 1) "Hukum dan Perempuan: Studi tentang Perspektif Aparatur Penegak Hukum di Aceh Utara" a book chapter in *Serambi Mekkah yang Berubah: Views from Within* (Jakarta: Alvabet 2010); 2) "Women And Divorce: Legal Justice Study of Societal And Judicial Perspective Toward Unrecorded Divorce in Aceh, Indonesia", *US China Law Review* (2015); 3) "Urgensi Kehadiran Hukum Keluarga di Aceh", *Mimbar Hukum Journal* (2017).

John R. Bowen

is Dunbar-Van Cleve Professor in Arts and Sciences at Washington University in St. Louis. He has been studying Islam and society in Indonesia since the late 1970s, and since 2001 has worked in Western Europe and North America on problems of pluralism, law, and religion, and in particular on contemporary efforts to rethink Islamic norms and civil law. Awarded a Guggenheim prize in 2012, he was named to the American Academy of Arts and Sciences in 2018. His most recent book on Indonesia is *Islam, Law and Equality in Indonesia: An Anthropology of Public Reasoning* (Cambridge, 2003). His *Why the French Don't Like Headscarves* (Princeton, 2007) concerned current debates in France on Islam and laïcité. *Can Islam be French?* (Princeton, 2009) treated Muslim debates and institutions in France and appeared in French in 2011. *A New Anthropology of Islam* from Cambridge and *Blaming Islam* from MIT Press appeared in 2012, and *On British Islam: Religion, Law and Everyday Practice* from Princeton in 2016.

Tutik Hamidah

obtained her doctoral degree from State Islamic University (UIN) Syarif Hidayatullah Jakarta in 2009. She is a Senior Lecturer at the State Islamic University (UIN) Maulana Malik Ibrahim, Malang, East Java. She has produced numerous publications (mostly in the Indonesian language) on Islamic legal thought with particular reference to women rights and gender issues in Indonesian contexts, such as *Fiqh Perempuan Berwawasan Keadilan Gender* (Malang: UIN Maliki Press 2011) and "Dialektika Teks dan Konteks dalam Metode Istinbaṭ Fikih

Perempuan Kontemporer" *Ahkam: Jurnal Ilmu Syariah* 13 (1) 2013. In addition to her position as Member of the Indonesian Ulama Council (MUI) of Malang branch, she has held various positions at her university including Vice Dean of Academic Affairs (2005–2009) before taking a position as the Dean of Faculty of Sharia and Law from 2009 to 2013. Currently, she is Head of the Institute for Research and Community Service (LP2M) of UIN Malang.

Abidin Nurdin

completed his doctoral degree in 2017 from the State Islamic University (UIN) Ar-Raniry Banda Aceh in Islamic Law. Since 2008, he has been a Lecturer at the Faculty of Social and Political Sciences, Malikussaleh University Lhokseu-mawe. He is also an active researcher at the Center for Education and Community Studies (PKPM) Banda Aceh since 2006. He has undertaken numerous research fieldworks and published a number of works that include book chapters, journal articles and textbooks on a variety of local issues in Aceh as well as on different topics of Islamic studies, such as *Syariat Islam dan Isu-isu Kontemporer* (Banda Aceh 2012) and "Contemporary Religious Movement in Aceh: (Review of the Rejection of the Syiah in Aceh)" *Journal of Islamic Civilization in Southeast Asia*, 6 (1) 2017.

Euis Nurlaelawati

is Professor of Islamic Law at the faculty of Shari'a and Law, State Islamic University (UIN) Sunan Kalijaga, Jogjakarta. She obtained her PhD from Utrecht University in 2010. Her research areas include the development and application of Islamic (family) law in Indonesia, judicial practices, and gender issues. She has published books and articles, including *Modernization, Tradition and Identity: The Kompilasi Hukum Islam and Legal Practices in Indonesian Religious Courts* (Amsterdam University Press, 2010); 'Training, Appointment and Supervision of Islamic Judges in Indonesia', in *Pacific Rim Law and Policy Journal*, Vol. 21 (1) 2012, 'Muslim Women in Indonesian Religious Courts: Reform, Strategies, and Pronouncement of Divorce', *Journal of Islamic Law and Society*, Vol. 20 (3) 2013; 'The Legal Fate of the Indonesian Muslim Women at Court: Divorce and Child Custody', in *Law, Religion and Intolerance in Indonesia*, Routledge, 2016, and (with Arskal Salim) "Female Judges at Indonesian Religious Courtrooms: Opportunities and Challenges to Gender Equality", in *Women Judges in the Muslim Countries: A Comparative Study of Discourse and Practice*, Brill, 2017.

Arskal Salim

is Professor of Islamic Law at UIN Syarif Hidayatullah Jakarta and also has an adjunct position at Western Sydney University, Australia. He received his

PhD from University of Melbourne, Australia, in 2006. His PhD thesis was then transformed into a book published in 2008 by Hawaii University Press: *Challenging the Secular State: The Islamization of Law in Modern Indonesia*. From 2006 to 2009, he was a postdoctoral research fellow at Max Planck Institute for Social Anthropology, Germany. Based on his fieldwork on religion and legal pluralism in post-tsunami Aceh, he wrote a monograph entitled: *Contemporary Islamic Law in Indonesia: Sharia and Legal Pluralism* which was published by Edinburgh University Press in 2015. His research interests cover: legal pluralism, political Islam, Islam and human rights, comparative constitutional law, and legal practices in Muslim societies, studied from the perspectives of Islamic studies, legal ethnography, sociology of law, and legal history.

Rosmah Tami

gained her undergraduate degree in 1997 from the State Islamic Institute (IAIN) Alauddin Makassar in Arabic and Literature. Her interest on textual analysis began when she was writing her masters thesis on Gender Relations in Sureq Galigo from the volume "Ritumpanna Walenreng" for the the department of Sociology and Anthropology of Newcastle University, Australia in 2002. She was a Fulbright scholar at the department of Comparative Literature of Pennsylvania State University from 2005 to 2007. She completed her doctoral degree at the University of Gadjah Mada in 2017 on Gramscian studies in Islamic popular literature in modern Indonesia. She currently teaches cultural studies, semiotics and comparative literature at the Faculty of Adab and Humaniora at State Islamic University (UIN) Alauddin Makassar. She also participated at MIWF (Makassar International Writing Festival) as a literary critic in 2018. Her current research focuses on various aspects of socio-political life in the local contexts, especially Gramscian studies and mythological studies in the area of South Sulawesi and Bugis Muslim diaspora.

Atun Wardatun

is Lecturer at the Faculty of Shari'a, State Islamic University (UIN) Mataram Nusa Tenggara Barat. She completed her PhD on Anthropology of Islamic Law from the School of Social Sciences and Psychology at the Western Sydney University, Australia, in 2017. Her recent publications include "Confirming Domestic Identity, Supporting Public Commitment (The Case of Tuan Guru's Wives in Lombok Nusatenggara of Eastern Indonesia)", *Musawa, Journal Study Gender and Islam*, Vol. 14 No. 2 (2015); "*Ampa Co'i Ndai*: Local Understanding of Kafā'a in Marriage among Eastern Indonesian Muslims" *Al Jami'ah Journal of Islamic Studies* Vol. 54, No. 2 (2016); and "Matrifocality and Collective Solidarity in Practicing Agency: Marriage Negotiation Among the Bimanese Muslim Women in Eastern Indonesia," *International Journal of Women's Studies*, forthcoming (2019).

Note on Transliteration

We have adopted an intermediate transliteration style, minimizing use of diacritics except when needed for clarity. Editors make substantive choices when transliterating and when creating glossaries, and we have chosen to give priority to local ways of writing and understanding word forms. Because all the authors are writing about Indonesia and use standard Indonesian transliterations of Arabic terms, we retain the Indonesian written forms (thus: hudud, talak). Nonetheless, in the Glossary we label some of these words, even when written in an Indonesian style, as Arabic (Ar.) to indicate that they usually are locally seen as Arabic, especially when they have a technical Islamic meaning (thus: ghairu muakkadah). Other words are labeled as both Arabic and Indonesian (Ar., Ind.) to indicate that they have an Arabic derivation and also are locally seen as standard Indonesian (thus: akad nikah, syariah). Some terms are from standard Indonesian (Ind.) and others are seen locally as belonging to local languages, and are so labelled (thus: co'i di pewe [Bima]). We realize that these are not cut and dry distinctions, but as long-term ethnographers of Indonesian Islamic discourse, we think we have arrived at a reasonable outcome.

Introduction

Studying Women's Access to Property

John R. Bowen and Arskal Salim

The past twenty years have seen an increasing degree of collaboration among scholars who share an interest in Islamic law but who were trained in diverse disciplines, from theology and law to anthropology and history. Major edited volumes attest to this new multidisciplinary approach to particular topics, whether the role of muftis (religious legal experts) and fatwas (scholarly opinions), the operation of courts across the centuries, or the broader social contexts of *shari'a* (see, respectively, Masud, Messick, & Powers, 1996; Masud, Peters, & Powers, 2006; Dupret, 2012).

This volume aims to support this multidisciplinary engagement with Islamic law, with a quite specific focus: Indonesian women's strategies to secure rights to property in Islamic legal settings. The spotlight on property allows us to look broadly at the range of factors shaping strategies and outcomes, from long-standing local cultural codes to recent Supreme Court circulars. The case studies examine different dimensions of this multi-faceted realm, with some authors concentrating on local cultural systems and changes, and others focusing on debates about how best to interpret Islamic law, or on practices of litigants, lawyers and judges in Islamic courts. Our contributors come from disciplines of Islamic studies, law, and anthropology, and they work in settings across Indonesia, from Aceh to Bima. We thus have a focused question, taken up across a range of social and geographical contexts in one country.

These cases concern inheritance, divorce, and related aspects of Islamic law. In Indonesia, these are the domains where Islam has had its strongest material effects, and where the relative claims of customary practices and Islamic norms produced vigorous debates and not a few armed conflicts over past centuries. Inheritance often was the focus. These debates and conflicts led generations of anthropologists and colonial administrators to describe inheritance systems in Indonesia, producing books on *adatrecht* (codified customary law) and, more recently, studies of state–law pluralism, or the coexistence of two or more formal legal systems that overlap in jurisdiction, of which the Minangkabau of West Sumatra long ago became the favoured study site (see von Benda-Beckmann & von Benda-Beckmann, 2006). Some of our contributors speak to this tradition of study, examining conflicts and changes across inheritance regimes and how these affect women's access to property.

© KONINKLIJKE BRILL NV, LEIDEN, 2019 | DOI:10.1163/9789004386297_002

Other contributors look at processes by which Islamic court judges make monetary awards to women as part of divorce proceedings, a topic that has been studied most extensively in Middle Eastern and North African countries. This regional emphasis is in part because of the high amount of the marriage gifts (*mahr*) in many of those countries, most famously in Iran. Payment only comes due if the husband divorces his wife, which means that the wife has a useful bargaining chip (Mir-Hosseini, 2001). Of course, some researchers have also studied this topic in Indonesia, but more emphasis has been placed on tracing changes in national family law.[1]

Why the focus here on women? Across the Muslim world, scholars have started from the local social and cultural structures that shape men's and women's access to resources, and found varying degrees of gender asymmetry. Islamic textual concepts play a role in providing justifications for men's control of households, of public and political roles, and of land and other forms of property. But from one region to another, Muslim societies also exhibit profound differences in gendered ideas and practices: one well-known indicator of the power of cultural forces remains the sharp difference in women's survival rates between South and Southeast Asia. Against these interwoven backgrounds of textual justifications and cross-regional differences in gender asymmetry, anthropologists have highlighted women's strategies for drawing on Islam to their own material advantage.[2]

Some of these studies highlight the importance of power, knowledge, and social ties in courtroom contexts, but they approach those contexts in differing ways. For example, studying divorce in Iran and Morocco, Ziba Mir-Hosseini (2001) emphasizes how litigants strategically represent their divorce demands and how judges seek to bring about the outcomes they personally prefer. She shows that all actors work strategically within the constraints of statutes and fatwas. Mir-Hosseini's work showcases a working judicial system in a classical social anthropological way, as a set of mechanisms within which people work to achieve ends; it also emphasizes the Islamic repertoire as interpreted by judges, muftis, and litigants. Arzoo Osanloo (2009) visits similar Iranian courtrooms but as part of a study of rights discourses. She shows how women's claims to be rights-bearers are nourished in Qur'anic study groups but also by the codification of Iranian civil law that makes explicit individual rights; they have multiple

---

1　For studies of courtroom awards, see Bowen, 2003; van Huis, 2016, pp. 167–193; Nurlaelawati, 2010. For the broader picture, see Feener and Cammack, 2007.

2　On textual justifications see Ali, 2016; Mir-Hosseini, 1999; on property strategies and kinship patterns, see Moors, 1995; Mundy, 1988, pp. 1–123; on demographic imbalances, see Sen, 1990.

pathways for asserting rights, not limited to the strategic manipulation of textual references carried out in the courtrooms (Mir-Hosseini, 2009).

Anthropological studies of judges and courts also examine extrajudicial ways of resolving disputes and regulating property transmission. Scholars trace women's strategies and outcomes with respect to specific regimes that shape access to property, such as systems of common property, patron–client relationships, property distribution rules, and kinship systems (see, respectively, Benda-Beckmann, 1979; Ilahiane, 2004; Peters, 1978; Mundy, 1988). Here careful ethnographic work has shown that a rule or category, such as those regarding women's rights to inheritance shares, conceals a multidimensional space of power and resources. Annelies Moors's (1995) important study of Palestinian women shows, inter alia, that inheriting property can be a mark of a woman's social status, indicating she is part of a wealthy, high-status family, or it can indicate she is in a weak situation and must claim property to survive – but even then, she is likely to lose the property to her more powerful brothers or cousins. Moors's study adds ethnographic substance to Pierre Bourdieu's (1977) well-known argument that 'following rules' explains little of the political economy of marriage or transfers of property.

These and other authors also discuss social changes that affect women's practical claims to property, including the effects of women's education and employment on access to property, in part through enhanced social capital (Chatty, 1996; Quisumbing & Maluccio, 2003), and, working in the other direction, processes such as commercialization, population growth, and concurrent increases in land value that make it more difficult for women to access and retain property (Gray & Kevane, 1999).

Indonesian Contexts

Over the past century, socio-legal change in Indonesia has followed a rhythm of gradual centralization and then sudden decentralization. If in the early 20th century, colonial rulers marginalized the role of Islamic law, by the end of that century a series of legal reforms had created a centralized Islamic judiciary with authority over matters of marriage, divorce, and, in ways that differed by province, inheritance among Muslims. In parallel, various local ways of resolving disputes were transformed by Dutch scholars and administrators into usable codes of '*adat* law' (*adatrecht*), each applicable in its own administrative region. After Indonesia's independence, both Islam and *adat* were reformed by Supreme Court rulings and other national legislation into positive law in the form of codes and rulings.

Although one can say that Southeast Asian societies enjoy relative gender equality compared to other regions – women and men work together in the fields, in child care, and in commerce and education – some tenets of Islamic law conflict with the general sense that women and men have equal claims on property and in married life. In the early 20th century, Islamic law was interpreted as offering women a post-divorce payment rather than a share of property, and gave men rights to initiate divorce not shared by women. *Adat* systems often gave only sons rights to land, although generally women had some inheritance rights, and in some societies inheritance and status were passed through women, although not necessarily controlled by women.

Beginning in the 1930s, women's groups demanded equal property rights for women and the reform of marriage and divorce laws. After independence, the Indonesian Supreme Court proclaimed that a new, post-revolutionary 'living *adat*' held the equality of men and women as a notable principle. Others tried to develop a new Indonesian tradition of Islamic jurisprudence, and they did so by pointing to the cultural specificity of Indonesian values and practices vis-à-vis the Arab world. Differences in the global sphere of Islam thus could justify innovation in Indonesian Islamic norms (see Bowen, 2003; Feener, 2011).

The major concern of the New Order Indonesian state was, however, to control and centralize. For Islamic law in Indonesia, three measures established the current system. The 1974 marriage law gave Islamic courts sole authority to recognize marriages and divorces for Muslims, including the husband's repudiation of his wife, the *talaq*, which in previous years he could effectively perform on his own. A 1989 law created a uniform set of jurisdictional rules for courts throughout Indonesia and in particular gave to Islamic courts jurisdiction – but not always sole jurisdiction – over inheritance matters, although the degree to which such courts have been used continues to differ greatly from one province to another. Finally, in 1991, President Suharto ordered that the new *Compilation of Islamic Law in Indonesia* be followed by all civil servants, including judges. The compilation consists of a set of rules concerning Islamic family law. With these changes, the officially mandated sources of Islamic law for resolving property disputes moved from selected books of fiqh to a new legal code.

Much recent scholarship on women's legal rights focuses precisely on these processes of *étatisation* of Islamic law (see Cammack, 1997; Nurlaelawati, 2010; Salim & Azra, 2003). This literature traces how the New Order regime preferred the unification of law by: 1) selecting only one of many available forms of Islamic jurisprudence and making it national law, 2) taking legal norms from various existing legal practices (living law) and ratifying them as positive law, and 3) compressing different legal provisions and processes into a single legal

INTRODUCTION

procedure. The state not only steered the processes and shaped the legislation but also had a stronger role than before (for example, in judicial granting of divorce). As a result, in court practice, many judges and justice seekers hold simplified views that 1) law is official and monolithic; 2) state laws are superior to and more valid than non-state laws, namely religious jurisprudence and social consensus; and 3) standardized legal procedures determine the outcome of legal processes. With all these views in place, law in many cases is regarded as produced by formal state institutions.

But real-life courtroom procedures have never been as clear-cut as this state-centric view would suggest. Judges draw on local cultural codes and their own views of morality and religion when weighing competing claims. Furthermore, other mechanisms of dispute resolution and property distribution have continued to operate in Indonesia's rural settings. Finally, the centralization of judicial power was perfected just as local governments were given the power to define more of their own political and cultural priorities, through regional autonomy laws that were passed soon after Suharto's resignation in May 1998. Political and fiscal decentralization gave rise to new cultural demands on the part of ethnic and religious groups regarding identity and self-government. These groups include local Islamic authorities, such as the Majelis Permusyawaratan Ulama (MPU or the Consultative Council of Ulama) in Aceh. In Aceh, the right of the provincial legislature to pass statutes based on *shari'a* was granted by the national Parliament in 1999 and 2001. We are only beginning to trace how these changes – legal centralization, and political and cultural decentralization – affect the aspirations and practices of women and men who seek legal remedies.[3]

The Organization of This Volume

This volume began as a research project focused on two provinces, Aceh and South Sulawesi, led by the editors working together with three local researchers in 2011–2013.[4] We then brought in other Indonesian researchers, all with

---

3 On the broad political changes see Holtzappel and Ramstedt, 2009; van Dijk and Kaptein, 2016; on the courts, see Lindsey and Butt, 2013; and on shari'a-based regulations, see Bowen, 2013.

4 Fieldwork was carried out under the auspices and with the support of the Andromaque research project (Anthropologie du droit dans les mondes musulmans africains et asiatiques), a three-year (2011–2013) project funded by the French Agence Nationale de la Recherche and led by Baudouin Dupret of the Centre national de la recherche scientifique. The project

research experience on the topic, by way of a workshop held at the Islamic State University (UIN) Syarif Hidayatullah, Jakarta, in 2013. Additional discussions, writing, and editing helped hone our thoughts and questions, now presented in this volume.

Each of the following chapter examines women's access to property in the forms of *mahr* (marriage gift), joint marital property, post-divorce payments, or inheritance divisions. Part one focuses on how local systems of meaning, norms, and power strengthen or weaken women's position and property rights. Atun Wardatun investigates a distinct form of marriage payment practiced among Muslims who live on the island of Bima, West Nusa Tenggara. Locally known as '*Ampa co'i ndai*', it literally means elevating one's own price, but technically the term refers to a practice in which the bride and/or bride's family pays all the wedding expenses, thereby raising women's status and countering 'traditional and common beliefs' about Islamic marriage payments at two levels. At the personal level, by reconsidering the *kafa'a* (suitability) of bride and groom, this practice lends bargaining power to the bride and/or her family. At the family level, this practice creates or enhances the social standing of both families, highlighting their interests in the future life of the bride by using the son-in-law to preserve both the bride's and their own status. The outcome of these actions and interactions can be seen in more or less access to property.

Rosmah Tami focuses on women's property rights among the Bugis and Makassar ethnic groups in South Sulawesi. She looks in particular at the concept of *siri*, meaning reticence, honour, or shame, both of individuals and collective entities such as an extended family. She discusses how the norm of *siri* serves as a means for women to have control over their property rights, and is articulated through particular features of wedding ceremonies. One of those is symbolically expressed in the form of a gift (locally known as *sompa/sunrang*, and is usually a parcel of land) presented to a bride. By studying a number of disputes over such property submitted to the religious judiciary of Makassar and Sungguminasa, Tami discovered that the local idea of *siri* creates both incentives and disincentives for Bugis and Makassar women to claim their property rights. On the one hand, a woman who upholds her *siri* will be able to negotiate the size and claim the amount of property presented during the wedding ceremony. On the other hand, she might fear that others would find

---

involved twelve senior scholars working on women's property rights in Muslim communities in four countries: Morocco, Sudan, India, and Indonesia. Project details are available at: http://www.agence-nationale-recherche.fr/en/anr-funded-project/?tx_lwmsuivibilan_pi2[CODE]=ANR-10-SUDS-0004.

her actions risky with respect to maintaining her family's dignity. That consideration might lead her to not seek control over property.

Part two focuses on women's perspectives and strategies. Tutik Hamidah studies how female activists in the two largest Muslim women's organizations in Indonesia, the Muslimat NU and Aisyiah Muhammadiyah, view the issue of the rights of children who are born to parents who are not officially married in a manner recognized by the state (as opposed to unregistered marriages). These rights include the recognition of a lineage relation and, in particular, the right to inherit property. A controversial decision of the Constitutional Court in 2010 now allows such children to receive an inheritance from their biological fathers. She considers a case submitted to the Constitutional Court reviewing a provision of the 1974 Indonesian Marriage Law that denied a legal tie between such children and their fathers. The case concerned a child who was born to Moerdiono (a former minister during the Suharto regime) and Machica Mochtar (a singer), who had an unregistered marriage. Hamidah finds that female leaders of both organizations appreciated the decision of the Constitutional Court, regarding it as a long overdue resolution that allows these children to inherit.

Analyzing legal processes governing access to inheritance cases in both civil and *shari'a* state courts of Lhokseumawe and Banda Aceh, Nanda Amalia examines female disputants' strategies in court and the extent to which these are helpful in securing their property rights. In particular, she discusses how the lawyers employed by female disputants to represent them interpret and make use of legal instruments to claim inheritance, and finds that these lawyers very often play decisive roles. She examines how lawyers construct facts and present relevant evidence, and how judges' decisions are influenced by lawyers' legal reasoning.

Part three of this volume focuses on the extent to which women's property rights are shaped by judges' assessment of submitted cases and their interpretation of legal texts. Euis Nurlaelawati examines judges' arguments for their rulings on women's demands for post-divorce payments, as seen in several case studies from religious courts of two districts in Banten province, Tangerang and Serang. She points out that the success of women in getting access to their rights has partly to do with the fact that many judges in both districts have been sensitive toward gender equality and have thus attempted to protect women's rights after their divorce. This sensitivity is found elsewhere in Indonesia as well, for example, when judges require the husband to bring post-divorce payments with them before finalising the divorce. But she also notes that many husbands cannot afford to make the full payment, and that it has been difficult to enforce monthly child support arrangements, not only because husbands may be financially burdened for many years, but also because divorced couples' relationships often have severely deteriorated.

Abidin Nurdin focuses on decisions made by Islamic judges about the amount of post-divorce payments to ex-wives. If Nurlaelawati generally discusses legal reasoning of Islamic judges in providing women with some divorce payments, Nurdin looks closely at how Islamic judges evaluate the wives' good or bad conduct during marriage to determine the amount of divorce payments. He shows that Islamic judges employed the concept of *nusyuz* (disobedience) to measure wives' conduct and allocated post-divorce payments based on this assessment. Four case studies from Banda Aceh and Jantho *shari'a* courts show that judges often emphasize wives' behaviours more than husbands' financial ability to afford the post-divorce payments. In addition, he includes a discussion on procedures to carry out post-divorce payments to women whose ex-husbands are Indonesian civil servants. Despite the existence of a law to regulate the marriage and divorce of Indonesian civil servants, some judges oppose this state regulation as contradictory to Islamic law. In their view, obliging male civil servants to share one-third of their monthly incomes with their ex-wives until they get remarried to new husbands goes against Islamic law and is therefore not enforced.

Arskal Salim investigates why and how marriage payments in two Indonesian provinces (Aceh and South Sulawesi) are transformed into disputes. He not only looks at the distinct meanings of marriage payments in both regions, but also examines the extent to which judges assess and accept evidence presented before the courtroom. A comparative analysis shows that while social status and hierarchy in South Sulawesi continue to be important, social strata in Aceh have changed significantly, and equal rights of spouses are more likely to be recognized. Disputes over marriage payments take place more frequently in South Sulawesi than in Aceh, which he argues has largely to do with the fact that marriage payments in Bugis and Makassar communities often take the form of land ownership transfers from a groom to a bride. This kind of marriage payment complicates the case especially because the land remains under the possession of the bride's parents and is seldom turned into a certificate of ownership in the wife's name even after years of marriage. A settlement of this type of dispute thus requires complex evidence to be presented before the judges: a marriage certificate, the husband's testimony, and the testimonies of the marriage registrar and witnesses who attended the wedding ceremony. Salim finds that judges did not accept a woman's claim of property ownership without seeing strong and relevant evidence.

INTRODUCTION

Closing Remarks

Across Indonesian Muslim societies, women both face obstacles and formulate strategies to gain access to property. In some cases, the obstacles derive from local cultural systems that make it difficult and socially costly to demand legal rights. But in others, we find that recourse to Islamic courts can give women access to land and other forms of property, not only because of the codification of Islamic law but also because of a widely distributed judicial concern with protecting women's rights.

More broadly, these studies show that it is only by following practices and cases at the local level that we can begin to understand how women and men fare in legal settings. Codes and compilations can then be seen as instruments deployed in order to achieve certain outcomes, not as summations of how things work.

Bibliography

Ali, K. (2016). *Sexual ethics and Islam: Feminist reflections on Qur'an, hadith and jurisprudence.* Oxford, England: OneWorld Publications.

Benda-Beckmann, F. (1979). *Property in Social Continuity: Continuity and Change in the Maintenance of Property Relationships through Time in Minangkabau, West Sumatra.* Den Haag: Martinus Nijhoff.

Benda-Beckmann, F., & Benda Beckmann, K. (2006). How communal is communal and whose communal is it? Lessons from Minangkabau. In F. von Benda-Beckmann, K. von Benda-Beckmann, & M.G. Wiber (Eds.), *Changing properties of property* (pp. 194–217). Oxford, England: Berghahn.

Bourdieu, P. (1977). *Outline of a theory of practice* (Cambridge Studies in Social Anthropology, Vol. 16). Cambridge, England: Cambridge University Press.

Bowen, J.R. (2003). *Islam, law and equality in Indonesia: An anthropology of public reasoning.* Cambridge, England: Cambridge University Press.

Bowen, J.R. (2013). Contours of sharia in Indonesia. In M. Künkler & A. Stepan (Eds.). *Democracy & Islam in Indonesia* (pp. 149–167). New York, NY: Columbia University Press.

Cammack, M. (1997). Indonesia's 1989 Religious Judicature Act: Islamization of Indonesia or Indonesianization of Islam? *Indonesia, 63,* 143–168.

Chatty, D. (1996). *Mobile pastoralists: Development planning and social change in Oman.* New York, NY: Columbia University Press.

Dupret, B. (Ed.). (2012). *La charia aujourd'hui.* Paris, France: La Découverte.

Feener, R.M. (2011). *Muslim legal thought in modern Indonesia.* Cambridge, England: Cambridge University Press.

Feener, R.M., & Cammack, M.E. (Eds.). (2007). *Islamic law in contemporary Indonesia: Ideas and institutions.* Cambridge, MA: Harvard University Press.

Gray, L., & Kevane, M. (1999). Diminished access, diverted exclusion: Women and land tenure in sub-Saharan Africa. *African Studies Review, 42* (2), 1–15.

Holtzappel, C.J.G., & Ramstedt, M. (Eds.). (2009). *Decentralization and regional autonomy in Indonesia: Implementation and challenges.* Singapore: Institute of Southeast Asian Studies.

Ilahiane, H. (2004). *Ethnicities, community making and agrarian change: The political ecology of a Moroccan oasis.* Lanham, MD: University Press of America.

Lindsey, T., & Butt, S. (2013). Unfinished business: Law reform, governance, and the courts in post-Suharto Indonesia. In M. Künkler & A. Stepan (Eds.), *Democracy & Islam in Indonesia* (pp. 168–186). New York, NY: Columbia University Press.

Masud, M.K., Messick, B., & Powers, D.S. (Eds.). (1996). *Islamic legal interpretation: Muftis and their fatwas.* Cambridge, MA: Harvard University Press.

Masud, M.K., Peters, R., & Powers, D.S. (Eds.). (2006). *Dispensing justice in Islam: Qadis and their judgments.* Leiden, Netherlands: Brill.

Mir-Hosseini, Z. (1999). *Islam and gender: The religious debate in contemporary Iran.* Princeton, NJ: Princeton University Press.

Mir-Hosseini, Z. (2001). *Marriage on trial: A study of Islamic family law* (revised ed.). London, England: I.B. Tauris.

Moors, A. (1995). *Women, property and Islam: Palestinian experiences, 1920–1990.* Cambridge, England: Cambridge University Press.

Mundy, M. (1988). The family, inheritance, and Islam: A re-examination of the sociology of faraa'id law. In A. al-Azmeh (Ed.), *Islamic law: Social and historical contexts* (pp. 1–123). London, England: Routledge.

Nurlaelawati, E. (2010). *Modernization, tradition and identity: The Kompilasi Hukum Islam and legal practice in the Indonesian religious courts.* Amsterdam, Netherlands: Amsterdam University Press.

Osanloo, A. (2009). *The politics of women's rights in Iran.* Princeton, NJ: Princeton University Press.

Peters, E.L. (1978). The status of women in four Middle East Communities. In L. Beck & N. Keddie (Eds.), *Women in the Muslim world* (pp. 311–350). Cambridge, MA: Harvard University Press.

Quisumbing, A.R., & Maluccio, J.A. (2003). Resources at marriage and intrahousehold allocation: Evidence from Bangladesh, Ethiopia, Indonesia, and South Africa. *Oxford Bulletin of Economics and Statistics, 65* (3), 283–327.

Salim, A., & Azra, A. (2003). Introduction: The state and *shari'a* in the perspective of Indonesian legal politics. In A. Salim & A. Azra (Eds.), *Shari'a and politics in modern Indonesia* (pp. 1–16). Singapore: ISEAS.

Sen, A. (1990, December). More than 100 million women are missing. *New York Review of Books, 37* (20), 61–66.

van Dijk, K., & Kaptein, N.J.G. (Eds.). (2016). *Islam, politics and change: The Indonesian experience after the fall of Suharto*. Leiden, Netherlands: Leiden University Press.

van Huis, S. (2016). The Islamic court of Bulukumba and women's access to divorce and post-divorce rights. In K. van Dijk & N.J.G. Kaptein (Eds.), *Islam, politics and change: The Indonesian experience after the fall of Suharto* (pp. 167–194). Leiden, Netherlands: Leiden University Press.

PART 1

Local Systems of Meaning, Norms and Power

∵

CHAPTER 1

The Social Practice of *Mahr* among Bimanese Muslims
Modifying Rules, Negotiating Roles

Atun Wardatun

Social anthropologists have long emphasized the importance of studying payments attendant on marriage (Evans-Pritchard, 1946; Goody & Tambiah, 1973; Moors, 1994). In many societies, these payments form a material outline of relations of status, economy, and gender. Furthermore, only by following payments across families, social classes, and villages can we grasp these complexities. The ramifications of material gifts and exchanges are not captured by statements of rules, but require an ethnographic study that allows us to capture considerations that often are not announced publicly (Bourdieu, 1977).

Such is surely the case in majority-Muslim societies. Islamic regulations on *mahr*, or payments made by husbands to wives as part of the marriage contract, are flexible in some aspects but rigid in others. While there are no exact standards as to the amount of *mahr* to be paid, or consensus on whether it should be paid upon consummation of marriage or deferred, there are, at least, three *mahr* principles that have been specifically addressed in Islamic texts and legal structures. However, these have been modified, extended, and complemented by social practices. The focus of this chapter is on the gap between these *mahr* principles and empirical practice, which has received scant scholarly attention, and in particular the *mahr* practices of the Bimanese Muslims of eastern Indonesia.

The first principle is that the *mahr* provider should be a man and, as stressed by all schools of Islamic law, this is related to a husband's unilateral right to divorce his wife (Al-Shan'ani, 1960). In practice, however, *mahr* is not always provided only by the man: through negotiations, it can be provided by either the husband (and/or his family) or the woman (and/or her family) or by both. In Bima, it is common for women and/or their families to provide *mahr*, locally known as '*ampa co'i ndai*', and it is viewed as a means to maintain family stability by discouraging extramarital affairs that could lead to divorce.

Second, *mahr* is an obligatory marriage payment, the only one clearly stipulated by religious law. Monsoor (2008) describes it as a religiously sanctioned obligation of grooms to provide property to brides, signifying a man's respon-

© KONINKLIJKE BRILL NV, LEIDEN, 2019 | DOI:10.1163/9789004386297_003

sibility to initiate marriage. In fact, *mahr* frequently accompanies other payments such as dowry or bride wealth, as well as many other types of local payment arrangements. Rapoport (2000) for example, writes that in early Islamic Egyptian marriage, there was *jihaz* or *shiwar*, terms that refer to dowry, a matrimonial gift brought by the bride into her marriage as a counterpart to the *mahr* referred to locally as 'shadaq'. In contemporary Egyptian Muslim marriages, *mahr* is overshadowed by other payments borne by the groom, such as *gihaz* (house and furniture) and *shabkha* (jewellery for the bride signalling the couple's engagement that becomes the wife's property once the marriage takes place) (Salem, 2001). Meanwhile, among Sasak Muslims in Lombok, eastern Indonesia, *mahr* coexists with *pisuke* (bride wealth) to compensate the *wali* (marriage guardian for the bride) for his approval of the marriage (*bait wali*) (Muslim & Taisir, 2009).

The third principle is that *mahr* is linked to the act of consummation. All four of the Sunni schools of law emphasize that a wife has the right to demand immediate payment of *mahr* after the marriage has been consummated and, if the husband wants to defer payment, she has the right to allow such deferral while remaining the sole recipient (Takim, 2012; Welchman, 2000; Monsoor, 2008). Practically, *mahr* is not only linked to marriage consummation and the unilateral right of men to divorce, but is also used by women as the main bargaining strategy for demanding or avoiding divorce, according to Mir-Hosseini (1993) based on her observations of proceedings in an Iranian court. Furthermore, *mahr* is also linked to the social background and status of brides and grooms. Moors (1994) for example, discusses how the deferral of *mahr* means different things for urban educated women and rural poor women. While urban women find deferred payment of *mahr* a problem, and even regard it as signalling women's dependence, poor rural women use such deferrals to strengthen their bargaining power with their family of birth should they divorce and need to move back to their parents' house. Likewise, in Makassar and Aceh in Indonesia, the primary function of *mahr* is to indicate social status and maintain family privilege (Salim & Bowen, 2013; Tami, 2013; see also Chapter 2 this volume).

It is important to note that with regard to the practice of *mahr* among the Bimanese, the aforementioned gaps between the principles and practices of *mahr* are not mutually exclusive. Thus the practice of *ampa co'i ndai* may occur with other marriage payments; such payments can become a status marker and be used by women to acquire power while maintaining gender roles. By focusing on the Bimanese local tradition of *ampa co'i ndai* I argue that the Islamic rules of *mahr* are, in practice, determined by various factors, including local tradition, family, and individual circumstances. Economic and social considerations shape how *mahr* principles are enacted among Bimanese Muslims. Negotiating with the bride and/or her family to provide the *mahr* payment is possible in this society because the social meaning of marriage and the marriage payment are that of a shared institution based on reciprocity (*kacampo fu'u*, literally translated as 'joint property'). Furthermore, this practice preserves the roles of men as economic providers and supporters, helps to meet women's needs for economic security and family stability, and maintains family status.

Patterns and Sources of Marriage Payments among the Bimanese

Men's provision of the marriage payment is commonly viewed as the only legitimate practice available under Islamic law, as if there was no justifiable Islamic alternative. Subhan (2008) suggests that it is possible for a society to insert another practice, such as giving property to the man, into *mahr*, but doing so is not considered to fall under the jurisdiction of Islamic law. On this matter, article 31 of the Indonesian Compilation of Islamic Laws codified in 1991 states only that the groom is obliged to provide *mahr* to his bride.

Mahr not only 'holds a central place in the legal structure of marriage' but also 'in the social practice of some Muslim communities' (Ali, 2006, p. xx). The practice of marriage payments has become a living tradition that is closely intertwined with cultural expression. Various meanings and patterns are evident among the diverse Muslim communities in Indonesia, in some parts accommodating Islamic doctrine but elsewhere deviating from normative prescriptions. The Bimanese refer to the marriage payment as: '*co'i*' (price or respect), which encompasses the *mahr* (*co'i di pehe* or stated payment), given as part of Islamic practice; land and/or house (*co'i di wa'a* or personal property), gifted as a cultural expression; and the expenses for the wedding party and traditional ceremony, called '*piti ka'a*' (spending money). When the bride pays the *co'i*, it is referred to as '*ampa co'i ndai*' (bride-paid marriage payment). However, in the marriage contract, the groom continues to be referred to as the sole provider of *co'i*. This is done to adhere to the Islamic code of conduct and so that the man does not lose face (compare similar disjunctions between public pronouncements and actual payments in the Bugis case, described in chapter 2).

Of these three types of *co'i*, only the amount of the *co'i di pehe* will sometimes involve consultation with the bride, as this will form part of her personal belongings. This is particularly true if the marriage is based on love and preceded by courtship, because the bride and groom will have agreed on how much and what kind of wealth they will each provide. *Co'i di wa'a* is normally assigned to the bride and groom by their respective parents, with the man bringing the house and the woman the land. *Co'i di pehe* is overshadowed by *co'i di wa'a*, as the former is often worth less than personal property and is thus regarded as less important economically. The amount of *piti ka'a* is decided by the bride's mother, as she is responsible for both receiving the funds and paying for the entire marriage ceremony.

Although the *co'i* provider is officially stated as the groom, both parties always contribute to it. The respective contributions of the bride and groom may vary, but at least four patterns can be identified, depending on the occupation and status of both parties:

a. When bride and groom are farmers and/or self-employed, and neither is a government employee, the groom provides the house and the bride the land. These are considered to be their respective *co'i di wa'a*, which they take back should the marriage end in divorce. If divorce takes place, the house is usually given to the wife to own; the husband's half can be put in the children's name or the wife may recompense her husband for it. This payment practice still takes place among farmers, and was common when subsistence farming was the norm and government employment was a rarity. The payment of *mahr* is commonly shouldered to the groom in the form of 5 to 10 grams of gold jewellery and/or a set of prayer equipment.

b. When the groom is a government employee and the bride lacks higher education and/or is not a government employee, she provides all the funds. The bride receives land as personal property from her parents, and the groom is not expected to provide the house. Men's access to higher education beginning in the 1960s allowed them to secure government jobs, which increased their status compared to women who still tended to work as farmers. In this arrangement, women provide payment to compensate for the economic security they will receive from their husbands' monthly salary, and also to establish and maintain their social status as wives of public servants. In such a marriage *mahr* is normally set between 10 and 15 grams of gold jewellery and a set of prayer equipment.

c. If the bride is a government employee and the groom is not (but may be a successful farmer, businessman, or other professional), the groom is primarily responsible for providing the *co'i*, a house, land, and furniture. The bride however still contributes to the wedding, as wedding celebrations in Bima are always held at the bride's family home. The bride and the groom still have rights to receive land from their parents respectively as personal property.

d.   If both the bride and groom are government employees, their *Surat Keputusan* (governmental decree of appointment) demonstrates they have a regular monthly salary to contribute to their new family. This pattern only commenced in the 1980s when women began to enter higher education and become government employees. If the bride's parents have productive land and the groom's parents have a house, these will be given to them as personal property. Both bride and groom contribute financially to the wedding party, as agreed by both parties. Both bride and groom, or just the groom, may contribute the *mahr* stated during the ceremony, depending on the agreement between them and both sets of families. The amount of *mahr* commonly paid is 15 to 25 grams of gold jewellery and a set of prayer equipment.

These four patterns of marriage payment among the Bimanese show that marriage is considered a joint investment, involving the bride, the groom, and both sets of families. This is clear from the practice of mutual contributions from the bride and groom and the parents' provision of personal property for each of them. The Bimanese accommodation of *mahr* provisions into their cultural context enables them to compensate for the particular 'social location' of the bride and groom and for their prospects.

There are key aspects to the negotiation of marriage payment that result in these patterns: mutual contributions, provision of *mahr* alongside *co'i di wa'a* and/or the *Surat Keputusan*, payment as compensation or *ampa co'i ndai*, and the special consideration of government employment. Mutual contributions refer to the bride and groom's respective financial support to the newly established family. The amount of contribution sought is determined by the occupational status of each party, which serves as an indicator of who is most likely to contribute the greatest financially to the marriage, regardless of gender. The Bimanese refer to this principle of mutual contribution as '*kacampo fu'u*' (joining of capital or property). The payment is seen as an attempt to gain respect (immaterial value) within a relationship, through the provision of mutually valuable benefits by both parties. In the first and fourth cases above, married partners of similar occupations (farmers with their personal property or *co'i di wa'a*, and government employees with their *Surat Keputusan*) provide mutual contributions, which are viewed as more significant for a new household than the *mahr* payment.

Mahr may well coexist with personal property and *Surat Keputusan*. In case (a) above, the *mahr* provided was less significant in value than the personal *co'i di wa'a* provided by the parents. Bima society has a well-established tradition of undertaking important discussions before marriage regarding what the bride and groom will contribute as their *co'i di wa'a* and how they will support the family economically. The *mahr* is not a key negotiation point when it comes to marriage payments. Likewise, in case (d) above, a less significant amount of *mahr* is still paid, even when a monthly salary is guaranteed by the *Surat Keputusan*.

Marriage payments may be made as compensation, as in case (b), where the bride will provide most of the funding to compensate for her lack of 'power' compared to the groom's status, both as a man and as a government employee. Here, *ampa co'i ndai*, or 'bride-paid marriage payment', literally means elevating one's own price. In the third case (c), where the woman is a securely paid government employee, then the man is expected to compensate for her position by providing her with *co'i*. However, women who are government employees rarely marry men who are not, so this pattern of groom-paid marriage payment rarely occurs. Only if the bride is nearing 30 years of age, and thus viewed as approaching spinsterhood, would she be willing to practice *ampa co'i ndai*.

The primary pattern of *ampa co'i ndai* is when the prospective husband is a government employee, usually in the army or police. Being a government employee is seen to offer many benefits, including economic, social, and family stability. Unlike businessmen who can only guarantee the economic needs of the family, or religious leaders who can only elevate the social position of the family within the village, government employees are viewed as promising a stronger bond of marriage as they are subject to government regulations that restrict the possibility of polygamous marriage and extramarital affairs. Therefore, the preference for a husband who is a government employee is motivated by three important factors, namely economic security, social status, and family stability.

It is assumed that if the man is a government employee, then he is a good person in terms of piety, lineage, wealth, and honour, since he has passed a government selection and screening process to acquire such a prestigious position. His family has spent much money on his education and in enabling him to acquire the job. To become a government employee, candidates do need to provide a declaration that they have never committed a crime, and part of the government entry interview inquires into the involvement of any family member in any illegal organization or social movement. This formal government process is taken as a guarantee that the husband is 'a fit and proper person' to build a family with and to establish and/or preserve family social standing and well-being. As one mother of a bride involved in *ampa co'i ndai* said, 'Who are we to judge a person when the Indonesian government believes him capable of taking care of this country?' (Maimunah, 58 years old). It must be said, however, that proof of good character is actually more theoretical than factual.

THE SOCIAL PRACTICE OF MAHR AMONG BIMANESE MUSLIMS

The economic responsibility and good character of the groom are indicators of his readiness to marry. In the past, there was a tradition called '*ngge'e nuru*' (literally, stay and follow) to determine this readiness, in which the prospective groom stayed at his intended bride's house, where the couple were not allowed to socialize but could only communicate with each other through the parents. This practice was a specific quest for the groom-to-be and a way for the woman's parents to find out more about the character of their future son-in-law (*rido katari*). The duration of *ngge'e nuru* was usually three months, during which time the bride's parents observed, tested, and trained him. He was expected to be good at farming, skilled at using the plough, and to demonstrate good characters, such as being honest, patient, and meticulous. The piety of the groom could also be assessed by his ability to recite the Qur'an and to perform the five daily prayers.

H. Karim (aged 63, teacher) recalled the groom-testing tradition that he had experienced:

> In the past, the father of the girl could test how honest and hard-working her prospective groom was. I experienced this *ngge'e nuru* when my father-in-law asked me to go to the river to fetch water. He would calculate the time it took me to perform this task and compare it with his own. I had been unaware that he was doing this but fortunately I made it, and he was convinced that I was the right man. If I had taken longer to do the task, he would have been doubtful.

The contemporary emphasis on a man's occupation as a government employee is a continuation of the tradition of *ngge'e nuru*, a way of establishing the ability of the groom to support the family and be of good character to ensure a harmonious family relationship.

Negotiating the Practice of *Mahr* and the Roles of the Bride and Groom

Ampa co'i ndai is a religiously and culturally based practice that has changed over time to accommodate modern shifts in employment patterns. The rule that the groom provides the *mahr* is maintained in the declaration of marriage but is modified in reality, even to the extent that the bride may well take over his role. Embedded in Bimanese *mahr* payment practices are the strategies wives employ to equalize their status with their husbands', to control family stability, and to maintain their family prestige.

Adapting Traditional Practices to Modern Circumstances

Ampa co'i ndai is not a new form of marriage payment, but rather a modification of *mahr*, which has long been given by Bimanese Muslims. It does however represent a slight modification of the basic form of Bimanese marriage payment, the *kacampo fu'u*. This change has occurred in response to the so-called modern bureaucratization of Bima society and the distinction made between the public and private spheres. I argue that the practice of *ampa co'i ndai* has both strong cultural values and religious bases. Both cultural and religious values are fundamental to Bimanese society, yet allowances can be made for reasonable adjustment to circumstances. Culture and religion are thus seen more as flexible ways and rules rather than rigid ones.

Ampa co'i ndai is part of the traditional life of an agricultural community, where strong bonds and close relations tie the members together. Nothing is considered to be a private matter; the community can always intervene. In an agricultural society, communal well-being is of primary interest and this can only be achieved by the participation of all members. Failure to participate is believed to bring about bad luck and disaster, which will put the whole community at risk. In the past, for example, there was a communal prayer for the welfare of the community and the prevention of natural disaster called the *do'a dana*; this was conducted by the entire community, including children, who sat down on the ground together and prayed before starting the planting. A communal approach still guides the local practice of *karawi sama* (mutual cooperation) where community members gather to jointly plant or clear one member's rice field, each member in turn being jointly assisted by other community members. The great effort expended in the wedding process is similarly seen as of communal interest, viewed not as a personal matter but a joint investment of the bride and groom and their families. Informants say the family and community are responsible for taking the couple through the process step by step (*kabua batu*) but without interposing their own interests into the couple's house (*uru batu*).

Marriage is arranged only for those deemed to be ready: both bride and groom should be able to economically support the new family while their respective families of origin provide the personal property, in the *kacampo fu'u* arrangement. This is connected to a longer tradition in which both parties were expected to demonstrate certain competencies (women in weaving, men in farming) that indicated their readiness. Both skills were equally valued as providing economic capital, rather than men being seen as occupying the prestigious public sphere and women the less valued domestic sphere. Neither sex was prevented from participating in the other's skills, and women in particular participated in farming.

In addition, the future bride and groom needed to demonstrate that their parents could provide land (from the bride's parents) and a house (from the groom's parents); these had to be physically shown to the other party before the union could take place. The furniture was to be provided by the man and the kitchen utensils by the woman, or they could agree to jointly provide what they needed.

Kacampo fu'u (joint investment) and *ngge'e nuru* (in-house screening) were two strong local traditions and they underlie the development of the practice of *ampa co'i ndai*. When brides and grooms were farmers and had similar educational backgrounds, women's weaving skills were seen as equal to men's farming skills. But due to the shift in employment away from agriculture into government occupations, and the expectation that men should achieve a high-status job as the head of the family and economic provider, society no longer expects male government employees to provide *co'i*, particularly when the bride does not have a similarly high level of education and is not a government employee. Expecting a man to fulfil all expectations of being a suitable groom and providing an appropriate *mahr* in such an unequal relationship is now viewed as exerting too much pressure on him, which could adversely affect the power balance within the family, especially when the woman's bargaining position is weak.

Thus, in response to modernization, including men's entry into the job market and the tendency for women to be distanced from the prestigious public sphere, Bimanese culture has provided a mechanism to maintain the balance of gender relations within the family by allowing women to bring their own economic resources into the marriage institution. When a government-employed potential groom approaches the prospective bride or her family, they know they can rely on him economically and are reassured of his personal qualities as a good partner. In this situation the bride is prepared to acknowledge the qualities and resources of this *arujiki* (gifted) husband by providing the *mahr* herself.

Ampa co'i ndai: *Women's Power, Social Status, and Family Prestige*

Two key terms that are frequently used in relation to the sharing of *mahr* payments are 'status uplifting' (*cua kana'e ngara*) and 'burden sharing' (*cua kaneo di rawi*). When a bride and her family contribute, they seek to strengthen their social status but not to the detriment of the groom's social status.

Ampa co'i ndai is commonly practiced by a couple of unequal status, to consciously balance the distribution of power between the husband and wife. By contributing to the *mahr* payment, brides compensate for their lack of social status, gain a bargaining tool within the family to control their husbands' behaviour (*aiba da saca'u adena*), and help maintain the stability of their new families. The practice remakes the bride's own status (*kaco'i weki ndai*) by paying respect to the status of the groom (*kaco'iku ngarana*).

A Way for Women to Acquire Power

Men exert specific privileges in Bimanese society: they can unilaterally decide to divorce, are less likely to be stigmatized if they have an extramarital affair, and may decide to have more than one wife. Women who employ *ampa co'i ndai* believe that these privileges or rights can be controlled so men do not indulge in them excessively. They believe that through this practice they acquire a balance of power that prevents them from being subordinated. Village informants, including those who have engaged in *ampa co'i ndai*, explained some of the motivations for this practice as including '*loaku na ntau fiki*' (so he has thoughts), '*baiba da sabe ra ne'e*' (so he avoids doing silly things), '*baiba da be ra ca'una*' (so he does not just follow his own will). The practice seeks to ensure that the husband will show consideration toward his wife and family and not just do what he wants.

The following example was related to me by Basir, an Indonesian soldier, and his wife, Fitri (both pseudonyms) whom I interviewed separately and then jointly. Basir had applied to join the army upon finishing high school, and acknowledged that the application process was quite expensive and his wife's family had helped him as part of their marriage agreement. He had met Fitri when she stayed with his family while attending the same high school in the city. Her family lived in a rural area and, as is common, sent her to stay in a relative's house in the city while she attended high school.

They had not fallen in love, but their families decided they should wed. The pressure on them to wed intensified when Basir and his parents decided they wanted him to join the army, rather than go to university. Serving in the army would help him secure a job quicker, and, providing he had enough money to get through the recruitment stages, he could have a stable job. After a long discussion with his parents, Fitri's family was willing to help, and it was agreed that they would marry later.

However, their marriage did not run as smoothly as planned. Once Basir was accepted as an army recruit, two years after they graduated, they were married, at only 20 years old. As they both admitted, neither had had the opportunity to enjoy life as a single person. This can affect a woman differently than a man, as a husband can have extramarital affairs, but a wife cannot. Basir said that he would never forgive her if she had extramarital relations, but, he felt that as long as he 'brings back the bottle he can share the filling of it', meaning that his 'manhood' is Fitri's but he could still have relationships with other women.

When I asked Fitri how she felt about this, she claimed that her husband was only joking, because he would never have the courage to behave in this way, and, even if he did, she would not believe it unless she caught him red-handed: 'If I do, I have the ace card, and I can let his parents know and report him to the army. Between them they have authority over his happiness and his job'.

While they both knew that Basir could still use his male privilege to be unfaithful to his wife, it was interesting to see that she knew exactly what actions she could take should he do so. When I suggested that the decision taken by herself and her family to practice *ampa co'i ndai* did not make any difference, since he could still use his power, she answered that if she had not contributed to the *mahr*, she might be in a worse situation in which she could not do anything. At least by employing *ampa co'i ndai* she believed that she rectified the imbalance of power between them and ensured he would not let her go without providing her with something.

Remaking Social Status

Personal and professional achievement is highly valued in Bima and achieving the security of government employment engenders huge respect, particularly if the man is employed as a teacher or lecturer, and even more so if a religious teacher or lecturer. People assume that teachers are well regarded by everyone in the community, and that they are knowledgeable people who can provide solutions to problems in everyday life. This is illustrated in the following stories of Ani and Aria, and Rahmi and Sam.

Both brides acknowledge their husbands' achievements in securing government jobs had been hard won. They were well aware of their struggles at university and were willing to provide the *ampa co'i ndai* payment because they did not want to financially burden their husbands any further. Ani and Rahmi felt lucky to have them as partners as they were good men, and because their own social status, as daughters of government employees, was maintained. Ani said, 'He is very similar to my father, as my mother said, and I am proud of my father', and Rahmi explained, 'My social status would decline if I married someone with no formal secure job, because my father is a government employee'.

At the time of our interview, Ani was 49 years old. She had graduated 22 years earlier from the Islamic university in the province, and she had married a classmate who had graduated the same year. Aria, her husband, had been a smart student who frequently helped his friends, including Ani, with their coursework. They became close, and his girlfriend at that time became jealous, leading to their breakup. Aria was from a poor family from Flores, East Nusa Tenggara, but because he had been identified as a bright student, a teacher had made arrangements for him to live with the teacher's sister's family in Bima so that he could attend the local high school and continue on to university.

The first time Aria met Ani's parents was at their graduation ceremony and her mother had asked more about him. On his way to visit his parents in East Nusa Tenggara a month later, he stopped by at Ani's house to wait for the ferry to take him home to his island. This enabled her parents to observe him more closely. Ani did not exactly know how the conversation began between her mother and him, but all she heard when he left was her mother saying, 'You know the way here now and you have to come back next time'. After he left, her mother began to discuss the possibility of Ani marrying him. Her mother said that Aria was like Ani's father, with a strong motivation to learn and a good personality, despite financial limitations, and told her, '*Aina tola arujiki ma taho*' (do not refuse good fortune).

The marriage was proposed, and Ani's family offered to provide all the funding for the wedding party and the *mahr*. Aria consulted his adopted parents and they agreed, and his birth family also accepted it because they did not feel they had contributed to his achievements and he therefore had the freedom to decide what he wanted.

This story is almost identical to that of Rahmi and Sam who also went to the same university; Rahmi's family was richer and had a higher social status than that of Sam, whose family were poor farmers. They began their courtship during the second year of university. Being the top student on graduation day, the fact that Sam was very smart was undeniable. The university hired him as an assistant lecturer after graduation, something that he had been doing informally while he was a student. Only one year after graduation he was appointed as a permanent state-employed lecturer at the university.

Maintaining Family Prestige

The Bimanese are proud of the social standing held by their extended family, which can help confirm an individual's good name. As one of my informants explained, it is good for men and women to marry within their extended family and thereby 'close the distance' (*kadeni ma do'o*) between relatives. Doing so prevents a man from becoming part of another extended family (*ntawipu laona dei dou*), and it consolidates the family name. This is illustrated in the following story of Jaka and Dija.

After graduating from high school where he trained to become a teacher, Jaka went to Kalimantan where he was told that it would be easier to be made a government employee. He stayed with relatives there and was fortunate to receive a permanent position after volunteering for two years at a junior high

THE SOCIAL PRACTICE OF MAHR AMONG BIMANESE MUSLIMS

school. Dija remained in her home village after finishing high school, choosing to improve her skills in bridal makeup rather than continue her education, because at that time, in 1970, women did not often go to university.

Jaka's and Dija's parents were second cousins but they lived in different districts in Bima. One day at a family gathering, Jaka's mother saw Dija, and thought she would be a good match for her son. Jaka's parents initiated the match by approaching Dija's parents, highlighting the fact that since they had spent much money helping their son Jaka find a job, Dija's parents would need to help fund the wedding if the match went ahead. Dija's parents agreed in that principle, but wanted to ask their daughter first, as they knew she had a boyfriend. They promised that they would try and persuade her. The marriage eventually took place with full funding from Dija's parents; as she explained, this was a '*karawi kakese*' (self-funded marriage). Their marriage strengthened connections within the extended family, and helped Dija's family improve their social status.

The goal of strengthening extended family connections is also clear in the story of Fauzi and Icha, both university graduates who worked as government employees. Fauzi, who was already employed as a marriage officer at the Kantor Urusan Agama (Islamic Religious Affairs Office), was happily surprised when Icha's parents approached him about helping her find a job. He had been interested in her and trying to find a good time to approach her, so her parents' request was, he said, 'a dream come true'. Their relationship began, and, although he did not proclaim his feelings, they showed each other gestures of love. A year after Icha got a job as a nurse, the marriage process was initiated. Her parents gave them a house to live in, the funding for the wedding party was shared, and Fauzi provided a *mahr* of 25 grams of gold jewellery. Icha and Fauzi have been married for almost eight years now with two children and clearly feel that their family is a good example of joining capital (*kacampo fu'u*) and enhancing family intimacy (*kadeni ma do'o*), family practices which they were told went back about five generations.

Conclusion

This study shows that to understand a complex social phenomenon such as marriage payments, we must attend to Muslims' ideas, emotions, and narratives in a particular place. Islam becomes part of these accounts in the form that local people give to it, in the ways they interpret sacred texts and Islamic traditions. The above examples of *ampa co'i ndai* illustrate that the *mahr* payment practice in Bima does not simply follow the Islamic legal text, which dictates that men should be the providers and women the receivers, but instead is adapted to individual circumstances. The ideal is also modified to fit with social practice, bridging 'what should be' with 'what could be' by providing the best solution to any given situation. Bimanese firmly hold to the belief that marriage is a joint investment (*kacampo fu'u*). If grooms demonstrate economic responsibility and good character, and have been screened through the *ngge'e nuru* tradition, the practice of *ampa co'i ndai* becomes possible in certain circumstances. This practice is also employed by some Bimanese women to enable them to acquire power in their marriage, which helps them maintain their new family's stability and their family of origin's status.

In this case as in so many others, it is only when we study both people's intentions and subjectivities, and also the broad social and economic context, that we start to see how social institutions of marriage work.

Bibliography

Ali, K. (2006). *Sexual ethics and Islam: Feminist reflections on Qur'an, hadith, and jurisprudence*. Oxford, England: Oneworld Publications.

Bourdieu, P. (1977). *Outline of a theory of practice*. Cambridge, England: Cambridge University Press.

Evans-Pritchard, E.E. (1946). Nuer bridewealth. *Africa: Journal of the International African Institute, 16* (4), pp. 247–257.

Goody, J., & Tambiah, S.J. (1973). *Bridewealth and dowry* (Cambridge Papers in Social Anthropology, no. 7). Cambridge, England: University Press.

Mir-Hosseini, Z. (1993). *Marriage on trial: A study of Islamic family law, Iran and Morocco compared* (Society and Culture in the Modern Middle East). London, England: I.B. Tauris.

Monsoor, T. (2008). *Gender equity and economic empowerment: Family law and women in Bangladesh*. Dhaka, Bangladesh: British Council.

Moors, A. (1994). Women and dower property in twentieth-century Palestine: The case of Jabal Nablus. *Islamic Law and Society, 1* (3), 301–336.

Muslim, M., & Taisir, M. (2009). *Tradisi Merari': Analisis Hukum Islam dan gender terhadap adat perkawinan Sasak*. Yogyakarta, Indonesia: Kurnia Kalam Semesta.

Quale, R.G. (1988). *A history of marriage systems*. New York, NY: Greenwood Press.

Rapoport, Y. (2000). Matrimonial gifts in early Islamic Egypt. *Islamic Law and Society, 7* (1), 1–36.

Salim, A., & Bowen, J. (2013). Changing patterns and different meanings of marriage payments in Indonesian two provinces. In A. Salim & J. Bowen, *Proceedings of the International Conference on Resistance and Accommodation: Law, women and property in contemporary Indonesia*. Jakarta, Indonesia: UIN Syarif Hidayatullah.

Salem, R. (2001). *Economies of courtship: Matrimonial transactions and the construc-tions of gender and class inequalities in Egypt.* Retrieved from PQDT Open: https://pqdtopen.proquest.com/doc/898822308.html?FMT=AI

Shan'ani, A. (1960). *Subul Al-Salam: Sharh Bulugh al-Maram Min Jam' adillat al-Ahkam/ Ta'lif Muhammad ibn Isma'il al-Kahlani Thumma al-San'ani; lil-Hafiz Shahhab al-Din Abi al-Fadl Ahmad ibn 'Ali ibn Muhammad ibn Hajar al-Kananani al-'Asqalani al-Qahir.* Cairo, Egypt: Dar Ihya' al-Turath al-Araby.

Subhan, Z. (2008). *Menggagas fiqh pemberdayaan perempuan.* Jakarta, Indonesia: El Kahfi.

Takim, L. (2017). Law: The four Sunni schools of law. In S. Joseph (Ed.), *Encyclopaedia of women and Islamic cultures.* Consulted online 07 September 2017 http://dx.doi.org/10.1163/1872-5309_ewic_EWICCOM_0111 First published online: 2009.

Tami, R. (2013). Siri and the access of Bugis Makassar women to the property rights in Makassar. In A. Salim & J. Bowen, *Proceedings of the International Conference on Resistance and Accommodation: Law, women and property in contemporary Indone-sia.* Jakarta, Indonesia: UIN Syarif Hidayatullah.

Welchman, L. (2000). *Beyond the code: Muslim family law and the shari'a judiciary in the Palestinian West Bank.* The Hague, Netherlands: Kluwer Law International.

Law and Regulations

Presidential Instructions No. 1 of 1991 in the Compilation of Islamic Law

CHAPTER 2

Siri and the Access of Bugis Makassarese Women to Property Rights

Rosmah Tami

On the second day of my fieldwork in the Makassar religious court, a humble but powerful village woman excitedly rushed into the registrar's office. The court officers had just recently executed a court order on two properties in the city, transferring ownership to her after a 15-year court battle involving first the Makassar religious court, then the South Sulawesi high religious court, and finally the Supreme Court. Her father had inherited the properties from his childless older sister, but they had been taken over by his sister's rich, adopted son. One day, the woman went to the son to ask for her father's share; in response, he insulted her for being backward, simple, and poor, and challenged her to sue him if she could afford it. The woman was enraged by his insults, feeling shame, known in Makassar and Bugis as '*siri*'. She became determined to defend her rights and therefore fought the case for 15 years.

The local Bugis and Makassarese languages are no longer common first languages among people in Makassar, who think of *siri* with nostalgia, believing it has been forgotten as a cultural notion. Yet, ethnographic fieldwork in Makassar and Gowa, including a focus group discussion held in Julubori and interviews with the directors of the Religious Affairs offices in the cities of Makassar and Sungguminasa, shows that *siri* remains an important consideration in social relations among Bugis Makassar people.[1] This chapter argues that in contemporary Bugis Makassarese society, *siri* both encourages and discourages women from accessing their property rights. To do so, after explaining the meaning of *siri*, I describe its location in Makassarese social structure, and discuss *siri* in several cases related to women's access to property rights.

---

1   Makassar people reside in Gowa, while both Bugis and Makassarese reside in Makassar. The two ethnic groups have intermixed through marriage, making it difficult to identify which cultural features are Makassarese or Bugis. Thus the term 'Bugis Makassarese' is used throughout this chapter.

The Bugis Makassarese Notion of *Siri*

There is no standard definition of *siri*, and people in South Sulawesi tend to explain *siri* based on what they have experienced in their family or environment. While *'siri'* literally means shame, Bugis-Makassar people use the term to refer to situations involving *harga diri* or self-esteem, *martabat* or dignity, *kehormatan* or honour, and *kebanggaan* or pride (Abdullah & Achmad, 2009, p. 7; Idrus, 2005, p. 39). According to Idrus (2005, p. 40), siri is also called *onro* or place which determines people social location (Millar, 2009) social place (Errington, 1989) and social standing (Errington, 1989) and social status (Robinson, 2001), which means that one should understand a place to where one belongs in relation to others.

These concepts are also found in other cultures, but what makes its local expression unique is the Bugis Makassar people's reaction when their *siri* is offended (Idrus, 2005, p. 40). An individual's sense of *siri* shifts when their honour is attacked or humiliated, or, in other words, when they are dishonoured. This is referred to as *'ri-paka-siri'* or humiliation, with the perpetrator referred to as *ma-ppaka-siri* (humiliator) (Ahimzah, 2007, p. 62). An individual or their family may also experience *siri* if they are the source of the dishonour. It is not unknown for a humiliated person to perform an action to defend or restore their *siri*; engaging in such actions is called *'jallo'* or running amuck. In such a state the individual may attack the person or people who had humiliated them. Should the attacker die in this retaliatory action, their death is highly respected and they are deemed to have died *mate rigollai* or *mate risantangi* (to die in sugar and coconut milk) meaning one dies in sweet and delicious death (Mattulada, 1985, p. 36; Hamid, 1985, p. 37; Idrus, 2005, p. 41)

Siri is also associated with an individual's dignity and humanity. An absence of *siri* means an absence of humanity, or a return to animal nature, and an individual who lacks *siri* is likened to a rat. *Siri* is seen as the essence of a human (Rahim, 2012, p. 139) and is linked to a human responsibility to defend one's honour, pride, dignity, and personal belongings (Mattulada, 1998, p. 91). This belief is expressed in a popular proverb from the Lontarak, the hand-written palm manuscripts of Bugis regulations and traditions: *'naiya tau de'e siri na; de lainna olokoloe, siri emmittu tariaseng tau, narekko de'i siri'ta, taniani tau; rupa tau mani asenna'* (A person who lacks *siri* is like an animal, because only people with *siri* are called human beings; if our *siri* disappears, our humanity thus disappears, what remains is just the human form) (author's translation).

Finally, *siri* is also related to the division of masculine and feminine roles in the family, and thus underlies interpersonal relations among the Bugis Makassarese (Idrus, 2005, p. 40; Ahimzah, 2012, p. xxiii). *Siri* involves a shared respon-

sibility: both men and women have a duty to protect or guard the family's *siri*.
Siri also refers to the female genitalia, where both shame and honour reside. A
husband must protect his wife's *siri*, and she preserves it and transfers it to their
children. Men protect the female members of the household from being humiliated by others or from bringing humiliation to the family. Women must keep
their family's dignity, pride, and honour by guarding their honour as women. A
mother will teach her daughters to guard the family's *siri*, while the sons must
protect the family's *siri*. A failed male protector is portrayed as effeminate and
an effeminate man is generally viewed as shameful. Respected Bugis Makassarese women receive many gifts upon marriage, which symbolise their *harga
diri perempuan* (female self-esteem) (Fokus Group Discussion Juluburi, 2012).
However, should a woman humiliate her family through *silariang* (elopement)
or *kawin sembunyi-sembunyi* (secretly marrying), she will not be showered with
wedding gifts but will be banished from her family for being *ma-ppaka-siri*
(humiliator); alternately, a bride's family may attack him for humiliating them
(Idrus, 2005, p. 41; Miswar & Setiadi, 2010).

Frequently, the *siri* of one person may envelop their whole family, especially
the men, whose role is to protect. A person does not bear *siri* individually, but
collectively within the family or group. This is indicated by the pairing the concepts of *siri* and *pesse* (Buginese) or *pace* (Makassarese). The literal meaning of
'*pesse*' and '*pacce*' is 'the feeling of pain in the stomach', as the stomach is the
place where brotherhood is bound. The pain of *pesse* connotes the idea of solidarity and empathy with others, which leads to solidarity. Thus, *siri* may also
be understood as a collective feeling underlying interpersonal relations.

Siri and the Social Location of the Bugis Makassarese Bride and Groom

The wedding ceremony is one event where social status is clearly marked, as is
evident in the amount and value of the gifts that are formally presented by the
groom's family to the bride that are called '*sompa*' by the Bugis and '*sunrang*'
by the Makassarese (but for simplicity are referred to as '*sompa*' in this chapter). According to some sources, who quoted the Lontarak, the giving of gifts is
an integral part of articulating the Bugis Makassar social structure. The social
location of the two families determines the value of the gifts, which then represent the nobility and honour of the bride and her family. Wedding gifts tend to
consist of the *sompa*, *mahar* (a gift from the groom himself to the bride), wedding expenses, and *erang-erang* (female ornaments). All these gifts come from
the groom's family or (as in the case of *mahar*) the groom himself. Today, wed-

ding expenses are often more than the *sompa*, for the bigger the celebration, the higher the social status it reflects. Generally, the higher the social rank of the woman getting married, the more gifts that are bestowed. Gifts, then, have both social and economic values.

According to Susan Millar (2009, p. 225) social relations among the Bugis are competitive and hierarchical, with individuals striving to achieve higher status whilst also seeking to protect their inherited privilege. Social status is a sensitive issue and often a source of conflict, causing people to pay careful attention when relating to others. Mattulada (1985, p. 56) explains that the *sompa*'s value is determined according to the bride's family rank; one must carefully consider the bride's social status so that the right gifts are given, as it may lead to *siri* or offence. If the bride is given more *sompa* than what she should, based on her social rank, it means she is highly appreciated by the groom and his family; if he is capable of showing great appreciation, it means that the groom has great power. However, the amount of *sompa* given may also be misrepresented. Often the sum of the gifted money is mentioned to the guests, without necessarily being shown to them, just to impress upon them the respect that was shown to the bride and the groom's power in presenting the gift. The goal is to impress the wedding guests with a display of respect for social location.[2]

According to traditional practice, a nobleman may marry a commoner, yet a noblewoman should only wed a nobleman because the bloodline is transmitted through the father. A commoner who marries a noblewoman is compared to a man who '*temei aju raja*', or urinates against a big tree; in other words, such conduct is considered highly inappropriate. Yet, such a marriage is not impossible, provided the man is powerful. The solution is known as '*melli darah*' (buying blood), which means that the man increases his social status through power he acquires in the form of wealth, intellectual talents, specialisation, or courage (Yani, 2007, p. 13). His power is demonstrated in the gifts presented to his noblewoman bride, which raise him to a similar level as her.

---

2 KUA or Religious Affairs officials in Manggala, Makassar, explained that the bride's family tends to demand more money for wedding expenses because the bride's extended family will receive the groom's extended family during the solemnization of the wedding and the wedding reception. This meeting of the two extended families and their friends is an important occasion to demonstrate their respective social locations. Thus the guests will drive their cars, and wear their gold jewellery and most expensive clothing to impress the other family (Head of officer KUA Manggala, interviewed on 25 January 2014).

Local Understandings of *Siri* as Related to *Sompa*

This field research revealed that the concept of *siri* is still very powerful and at the root of many family conflicts taken to the religious courts of Makassar and Sungguminasa. Even though an absence of *sompa* may be problematic, some wives do not receive a valuable gift from their husband. The family's concern that this might happen is reflected in the popular saying, '*Aja lalo muancaji makkunrai tenri-pa-bokongi*' (Don't become a woman without a ransom). The term '*makkunrai tenri-pa-bokongi*' describes a woman whose groom does not attempt to provide *mahr*, *sompa*, or any other gift at the wedding. It indicates that the bride and her family lack the power to negotiate a respectable *sompa*, the symbol of a woman's honour. It also implies a loss of honour or dignity on the woman's part due to immodest behaviour.

During my field research visits, when men and women were questioned about *sompa*, most claimed it is a symbol of social structure and some also said it is a symbol of woman's dignity. Some expected the *sompa* to be paid in the form of *real* or *reyal*, a pre-colonial Spanish currency, others held that it should be in the traditional form of valuable goods or property, and others expected both. Most stated that respected women should be given *sompa*, and that the absence of *sompa* indicates a lack of respect. Therefore, the presentation of *sompa* at the wedding ceremony is crucial (Head officer KUA Kassi, interviewed in Makassar on 25 January 2014)

Although many women said they had received *sompa*, some could not exactly explain what they had received. In some cases, married women tended not to be concerned about their *sompa*, as they had not been present during the *mappettuada* (pre-wedding negotiation). Nurfaidah Said (2002, p. 66) writes that when women were asked whether they had received *sompa*, they all answered that they had but their answers revealed some uncertainty. For example, they said: '*Saya dikasi tau sama tanteku kalau ada sompaku*' (My aunt said that I have *sompa*), '*Tautoaku, ammakku pawwangnga kana nisunrangnag tana*' (My parents, my mother said that my *sunrang* is a piece of land), and '*Saya di Makassar waktu itu. Saya kuliah. Semua* [sompa/sunrang] *itu diputuskan oleh orang tua dan keluarga. Nanti hari pesta baru saya pulang*' (I was in Makassar at that time. I was studying. My family and my parents decided it all. I returned home the day of the wedding).

Others answered that they were present and knew about their *sompa*, but had stayed silent during the negotiations. For example, Nur (pseudonym) recalled:

> Saya dengar semua pembicaraan orang, disebut satu persatu, mulai dari *sompa*, uang belanja, *lekocaddi, leko lompo, cincin*. Pokoknya saya dengar

SIRI AND THE ACCESS OF WOMEN TO PROPERTY RIGHTS   35

semua. Malahan saya yang bikinkan air panas untuk tamu. [...] saya ikut
saja apa yang mereka putuskan oleh keluarga [I heard all the conversation, it was mentioned one by one, from the *sompa*, wedding expenses,
small food box, jewellery box, ring. Basically, I heard it all. I even served
them hot drinks. I just followed what my family had decided].

While the *sompa* is announced during the wedding solemnisation ceremony,
the bride is not present at that moment because she is secluded in a wedding bedroom, waiting to be picked up by the groom after the ceremony. The
sompa is formally accepted by the bride's father or his representative. However,
sometimes *sompa* are recorded on the marriage certificate and the amount
mentioned during the ceremony.[3] Women's passivity regarding their *sompa* is
encouraged by Bugis Makassarese tradition, which prefers women to be mod-
est and not demand *sompa*. Some Bugis women admitted to receiving *sompa*
but never saw it or asked for a deed of ownership for fear of being considered
makkunrai mangoa (greedy women) or *makkunrai makurrang siri* (women who
lack honour). When asked if they knew the amount of rice their *sompa* land
produced, Bugis Makassarese women gave answers such as: '*Ajjalalomakku-
tana, masiri memenni*' (Oh, please, no, I have never gone to ask that, shame
on me), and '*Ada tapi tidak boleh ditanyakan, malu-maluki, nanti kita dibilang
serakah*' (There is *sompa* but it was inappropriate to ask about it. It would cause
shame. I do not want to be considered greedy).

The connection between *sompa* and *siri* is clear: *sompa* announces the family's location to society, but married women prefer not to mention it to protect
their *siri*. The *sompa* is celebrated as a marker of the family's dignity and pride,
while the bride's silence is a way to preserve the honour of her new family
and also her birth family. The honour of the woman also reflects the honour of
the husband as head of the family. This reflects the complex position of Bugis
Makassarese women within the structure of society and the crucial role played
by *siri* in shaping social relations. The cases below further explore the connection between *sompa* and *siri*.

The Social Location of Sompa *and Its Relation to* Siri

The following case from the Makassar religious court concerns the wedding of
Becce and Baso (pseudonyms). The bride Becce came from a family of Makas-
sar intellectuals and her mother from an aristocratic family. The groom Andi
Baso was born to a noble family in Mandar, West Sulawesi. When their wed-

---

3   See Makassar Religious Court Decision.

ding was being planned, the *sompa* was a topic of heated negotiation due to the statuses of the two families. Becce's family argued that the *sompa* should constitute valuable property, as would be expected as a gift among the elite and aristocracy. The negotiation appeared successful, and the keys of a house were formally displayed and loudly announced to the crowd who witnessed the ceremony. Becce officially accepted the house by visiting it on her wedding day in her bridal costume. All her relatives felt respected by the generous gift, which marked and demonstrated the honour, dignity, and pride of their family.

After two years and the birth of a daughter, the marriage ended. It was at this point that the *sompa* caused problems. Sometimes a husband may take the *sompa* back to his parents, but if the couple have a child, the *sompa* remains for the child. However, despite wedding documents, including photographs, a video recording of the *sompa* announcement and presentation, and also letters of agreement, Andi Baso and his family insisted there was no *sompa* in the form of a house. Andi Baso's witnesses in court stated that the house that had been announced and shown at the wedding was not intended as *sompa*. They further claimed that Becce's mother had agreed to this, in effect creating a ruse to impress people regarding the power and the social location of her family.

This is a common problem in Makassarese and Bugis society and the subject of gossip. Sometimes *sompa* is presented just to impress people, and sometimes even the same property is presented as *sompa* at one wedding and then at other weddings (Judge Sahidal, interviewed in PA Makassar 28 June 2011). If a woman receives only a small gift, people may gossip about her possible misconduct. However, when a large gift is provided, it is a source of pride and celebration for the whole family. In Becce's case, many witnesses testified they had heard and seen the house presented as *sompa*, and documentary evidence was provided. Yet, Judge Syahidal from the Makassar religious court understood the situation and tradition well, deciding to accept Andi Baso's defence and pronounce that the house was not *sompa* (Judge Sahidal, interviewed in PA Makassar 28 June 2011).

Such cases are common enough in both the Gowa and Makassar regencies that many Religious Affairs officers request that those planning to marry should detail the *sompa* and dowry in a letter of agreement signed by the local village chief. Nevertheless, this letter lacks legal force unless it is notarised by a law firm, which many people are unwilling to have done. As a consequence, conflicts like the one between Becce and Andi Baso often occur.

The Makassar religious court approved Becce's claims for child support and *mut'ah* (gift of consolation). Andi Baso objected to that decision and unsuccessfully appealed to the South Sulawesi high religious court. The court determined that Andi Baso should still pay Becce's *mut'ah* and child support for his daughter. Becce's aunt claimed that Andi Baso had not met his legal obligation to support the family, although they had not reported him to the police. Becce's best friend Ifa also testified that Andi Baso had refused to pay child support (Ifa 26 years old, Becce's best friend, interviewed 20 September 2012).

When the head of the South Sulawesi high religious court heard that Becce had not yet received any money from Andi Baso, he said that Becce should inform the court so that Andi Baso could be forced to pay according to the regulations. Yet, he admitted that the *sompa* mentioned by the Makassar religious court was not mentioned by the higher court. Dropping his voice, he said further that the case was a complex one, as the husband and wife had not been frank about the age of the daughter. The daughter's birth certificate had not been presented in court and the other information presented was not consistent about the daughter's age. It was not directly stated that Becce was pregnant when she married, but there were questions as to why the daughter's true age had been hidden (Interview with Ketua PA Makassar, 9 Juli 2012). Based on other documents and Andi Baso's father's testimony in court, the marriage appeared to have been somewhat forced.[4] This helps to explain Becce's relative silence in court and her unwillingness to force the issue of financial support. Her silence helped maintain her family's *siri*, although it blocked her access to financial support.

The Social Location of Siri in Inheritance

Case 0390/Pdt.G/2011/PA Makassar was filed in 2011 at the Makassar religious court by Ibu Hajjah Indo, mother of Rusli. Rusli, who had passed away in January 2011, had married three times, each time claiming to be single.[5] He had a teenage daughter, Tenri, by his first wife, who was not identified in court. He had three children, Dewa, Arini, and Eny, by his second wife, Mus. His third wife Nana had given him no offspring. At the time of his death Rusli apparently owned a number of properties, including a successful garage that he ran with his brother, Awing. The case was a dispute over the control of his property, which had been taken over by the second wife, Mus, who had sacked Awing. Rusli's family had been greatly upset at Rusli's secret third marriage to Nana, Mus's control of the property, and the dismissal of Awing. Rusli's mother, his sister, his teenage daughter, and his third wife together sued Mus for an equal share of the inheritance. After four hearings at the Makassar religious court, the judges concluded that there was insufficient documentation to support their

---

4   Makassar Religious Court (PA Makassar, 2011).
5   The summary here is taken from Case No. 0390/Pdt.G/2011/PA-Mks.

claim. The family hired a famous lawyer and filed a new suit in the same court in November that year, Case No. 1575/Pdt.G/PA Makassar, which was resolved in 2013.

This case documents reveal that Nana, Rusli's third wife, did not refer to any *sompa* given her by Rusli in court. Often *sompa* is absent in illegal, elopement, or polygamous marriages because there is little room for the woman's family to negotiate for such property. Rusli's sister, Tia, admitted that her brother had only introduced Nana to his brother Awing, which meant that the union of the two extended families of Rusli and Nana had not been celebrated in a big wedding. Nana only began to get close with her husband's family after being persuaded by Awing to access her rights as a third wife (Interview with Tia 49 years in PN Makassar, 13 November 2013).

Although she was his third wife, Rusli's sisters and brothers considered Nana to be the one who had brought him good fortune, as she had taken good care of him, unlike his second wife, Mus, who worked as a civil servant outside Makassar. After marrying Nana, Rusli's business grew successful, his garage developed quickly, and he bought many houses, cars, and land. Rusli's mother, brother, and Nana took other legal action against Mus, after failing to persuade her to share the property left by Rusli (Tia, 2013).

Tia, Rusli's sister, who spoke on her mother's behalf, stated that they felt humiliated by Mus's attitude, as she seemed not to take them seriously, was unwilling to meet them, and only came to court to cancel the hearing. Tia stated in court:

> Kita juga malu-malu pergi ke pengadilan setiap minggu begini, jama-jamang aga iyyae, tapi kita kasiang sama ponakan, kita memperjuangkan-nya. Ia berhak, istri kedua itu tak punya rasa malu, makanya kita harus perjuangkan [We feel embarrassed to be here in court every week; you see what kind of business is this? But we feel pity for our niece, we have to fight for her. She has rights, the second wife has no sense of shame, so we have to fight.]
>
> Tia 49 years, Interview 2013

According to Tia, Mus invited them to meet at a coffee shop in the city, which the family considered to be humiliating and inappropriate, as family problems should be discussed at home, not in a public space. After failing to agree on a meeting, and feeling sympathy for Tenri, Rusli's eldest daughter, his mother and his third wife united in a second legal action to take back what they considered to be their rights. Defending rights is a large part of *siri* practice of the Bugis Makassarese; it is an obligation. In the family's view, Mus lacked any sense of *siri* because she was greedy and had taken control of all of Rusli's property, blocking their access to it and thereby damaging the family's *siri*. It was their sense of *siri* that gave them the courage to attend the court hearings, together with feelings of *pesse* or sympathy in solidarity with Tenri.

After several complicated hearings, the case was eventually resolved in the Makassar religious court in 2013. The judges decided that Nana, the third wife, was not entitled to receive an inheritance, as their marriage was considered legally flawed according to state law. Documentary evidence revealed that Rusli had claimed to be a bachelor when he was planning to marry Nana, and was thus registered at the Religious Affairs Office as a single man. The judges were bound to declare the marriage illegal by state law, despite it being legal under religious law. As the judges had to consider both religious and state law in reaching a decision, they resolved to position Nana as if she were an adopted child, who under the Islamic law of inheritance is entitled to receive a *wasiah wajibah* (an obligatory bequest). She was awarded one-third of the joint property, rather than the 50 per cent of property as a legally married wife. One of the judges, Dra. Hj Siti Fatimah M.Ag, explained their decision was informed by considerations of Nana's support of Rusli when he was alive and sympathy should she not receive anything from the marriage.[6]

The second wife was not satisfied with this second decision from the Makassar religious court and appealed to the South Sulawesi religious higher court. This court determined in 2013, under decision 080/Pdt.G/2013/PTA.Sulsel, that the award of the *wasiah wajibah* was inappropriate, a decision that extinguished Nana's rights as third wife to one-third of the joint marriage property. She was not considered to be legally married, despite her marriage to Rusli having fulfilled all the requirements of *shari'a* law, and was thus not considered to be a legal heir. The judges of this higher court awarded Nana rights to the small, cheap house where she had lived with Rusli and the cheap motorcycle he had bought her. The judges did not find these to be part of Rusli's estate, but rather a *mut'ah* or consolation; they viewed her marriage to Rusli as similar to *nikah mut'ah*, or temporary marriage.[7]

Meanwhile, Rusli's mother and his daughter Tenri had their property rights legally recognized according to Islamic inheritance law. His mother and Nana did not take any further legal action, having been told by their lawyer that the higher judges' decision was correct. Rusli's second wife, Mus, appears to have

---

6   Case No. 1575/Pdt.G/2011/PA-Mks.

7   Makassar high religious court Decision No. 080/Pdt.G.2013/PTA-Mks.

won the case, having prevented Nana from being considered a legal wife due inheritance rights. Nana was left legally disempowered and culturally shamed for taking another woman's husband in a secret marriage.

A Case from the Women's Association for Justice and Legal Aid

I interviewed another woman, named Ija (pseudonym) whose husband divorced her without her knowledge or permission. She was a high school graduate but not formally employed when I met her, and her husband had worked in Jayapura while she remained in Makassar with their three children. He filed the divorce papers in the Makassar religious court with her falsified signature and a woman pretending to be Ija. An acquaintance who worked there told Ija about the matter and Ija fought to save her marriage, only to discover that her husband planned to soon marry a second wife. Ija recounted her actions on the wedding day:

> *Saya ke sana mengamuk, tetapi saya telpon sepupuku dulu yang kapolsek dan ia meminta saya melapor polisi, saya datang bersama polisi* (I went there to the wedding in a rage, but I first called my cousin, who used to be a local police chief, and he asked me to report to the police. I came with police officers).
>
> Ija, 36 years divorcee, interviewed in LBH-APIK Makassar on 13 October 2012

As previously explained, Bugis Makassarese react strongly when their sense of *siri* is offended, and attacking those who have caused humiliation is seen as an acceptable response (*jallo* or running amuck). As Mattulada (1985, p. 61) emphasises, *siri* is tightly bound to the individual's dignity as a human, which means they have the responsibility to defend their honour, pride, and personal belongings. In this case, Ija's rage prompted her to attack her husband and his new wife at their wedding reception to restore her pride. Ija's actions both impressed and disturbed many people, especially the two families who were uniting in marriage who experienced *siri* from this episode. It led to heated conflict and the husband was arrested and jailed for several months. As Ija related her experience, she frequently smiled and sometimes laughed; no sadness shadowed her face. 'A woman must be powerful to protect the children', she stated and continued:

> *Waktu itu saya sudah tidak peduli lagi apa kata orang tentang saya, yang kupikir itu anak-anak. Anak-anakji, disitumi saya berjuang* (At the time I

no longer cared what people thought about me, I was just thinking about the children. It was the children's rights I fought for).

Ija, interview on 13 October 2012 in LBH-APIK Makassar

Ija found the Women's Association for Justice and Legal Aid (Lembaga Bantuan Hukum Asosiasi Perempuan Untuk Keadilan, LBH-APIK) at the right time, when she was alone and devastated. One of the main civil society organizations assisting women across Indonesia, LBH-APIK helped and advised her regarding the submission of her documents and also provided her protection from her ex-husband's intimidation. With their help, she was able to properly take care of her divorce and gain access to joint marital property. She forced her husband to agree to provide her with a house and regular child support payments. Ija said it was difficult at first to obtain child support, as her husband had already remarried, but she said that LBH-APIK worked closely with her every step along the way. Furthermore, they also provided her with counselling to help her recover from the shock of her divorce and her husband's remarriage. After the divorce she was faced with the reality of being a single mother of three children whom she had to feed and educate. Now she owns her own house and works as a volunteer for LBH-APIK. Her ex-husband's family sometimes provides support, but her husband's new wife sometimes also intimidates her.

Ija is proud of herself. Her actions towards her ex-husband were not intended to humiliate him but rather to save her family and her own *siri* or self-esteem. She felt that any humiliation her ex-husband, his new wife, and their families felt by her disruption of the wedding was deserved due to their deceit. Ija stressed that her actions were to defend her rights, as it is honourable to fight for one's rights and protect one's family and children. With the help of LBH-APIK, Ija was able to follow the procedures required to win support for herself and her children. Their counselling also helped her to control her emotions and follow a legal course of action to attain her rights, rather than *jallo*, which might lead to further conflict.

Identities, Pride, and Women's Access to Property

The case studies show that social identities and values of siri can play a variety of roles depending on the events in question. Baso and Becce's wedding is an arena where cultural identities are marked or remarked. They drew on the older logic of gift-giving, social location, and the value of *siri* precisely in order to secure and reassure their modern existence. A big expensive wedding signified their social location in a material way that could be read by a multicultural urban society. Here, *sompa* is the cultural operator that helps clearly define and signal that location, and thus is connected to *siri*. *Sompa* brings honour and respect, signalling women's dignity and men's power; its absence brings the opposite. The importance of *siri* seems to be strengthening, as it empowers women to negotiate to gain access to property.

The family of Rusli's mother also drew on the logics of material goods and *siri* as part of a strategy to gain access to their share of the inheritance left by the late Rusli. They also reconciled with the daughter of the first wife, and with the third wife whom they had never met, to involve them in realizing their future goal, namely accessing Rusli's wealth. Their reconciliation to the past was surely provoked by a conflict with their present realities, the blocked accessed to the inheritance. *Siri* supported all the parties in uniting, and uniting was motivated by this material goal. The women of Rusli's family united to prosecute Mus, who was unwilling to share Rusli's inheritance. His mother and her family attended every court hearing to provide support to Nana, the third wife. Being *ripa-kasiri* (humiliated) seems to have been an inspiration and source of energy to bring the case to court. Yet, after his mother and her family gained their share, they stayed silent when Nana lost her part of the case, due to her weak legal and cultural status from marrying Rusli without his second wife's approval. Indeed, this visit to the past brought back the past story of the late Rusli and his third wife. Some stories that had been covered over but that now were re-opened left shame, and legal consequences.

But highlighting *siri* may discourage women from accessing their property rights, when the loss of *siri* leaves women powerless. It retains a mysterious and sacred signification, often in the context where the precise nature of the objects promised or given is kept obscured. Most of the married women I interviewed acknowledged that they had received *sompa* but they could not identify it, a pattern that reveals the significance of *sompa* for social and moral status. For some, if *sompa* is absent, the honour and respect of both families may be threatened. The material absence or existence of *sompa* is sometimes a family secret, and women are expected to remain silent after the announcement of *sompa* at their wedding ceremony and not disclose whether it actually exists. *Sompa* can be a complicated cultural practice, as it represents a valuable property marking the social location of the bride's family but one that can be reneged upon by the groom's family. Thus, *sompa* may remain unclear until the family has a problem, such as separation and inheritance. Some try to explain the logic behind *sompa* by reasoning that it binds the wife and husband, remaining the property of the family rather than being sold. It is passed down through the male from generation to generation, thus connecting them to their origin as well as identity.

In contemporary society, the economic and social value of *sompa* dominates its cultural value. A need to mark social location may direct some people to falsify the existence of *sompa* in a wedding. People may not be aware of the dishonour that may result from this falsification, as was apparent in the case of Baso and Becce. Moreover, this may also prevent women from accessing marital property rights following separation. *Siri* can be thought of as a cultural support that protects women's access to property, yet may also be a means for manipulation, using women's honour for reasons of social status. As evident in the heated negotiations conducted before Besse and Baso's wedding, the ceremony was clearly intended to demonstrate the honour of the family and their daughter. Here, *siri* should be interpreted as *kebanggaan* (dignity) rather than *kehormatan* (honour), as the former tends to have a more material interpretation whereas the latter is considered more spiritual in nature.

Conclusion

The above discussion demonstrates how the concept of *siri*, supported by traditional practices, in particular the transfer of property as *sompa*, helps define human existence in terms of dignity, honour, self-esteem, and pride in South Sulawesi. And yet valuing and acting in terms of *siri* can have quite distinct consequences for women, depending on the material and status positions of the families and individuals concerned. As Annelies Moors (1995) demonstrated for Palestinian women, property rights may have multiple, and sometimes opposed, material effects. To understand these or other cases, we must return to the culturally specific notions and emotions that guide people in their everyday lives: power and resources, but also pride and dignity, shape actions in locally specific ways.

Bibliography

Abdullah, H. (1985). *Manusia Bugis Makassar*. Jakarta, Indonesia: Inti Idayu Press.

Abdullah, H., & Achmad, A. (2009). Siri: Kearifan budaya Sulawesi Selatan. In A. Hamid (Ed.), *Siri: Kearifan Budaya Sulawesi Selatan* (pp. 1–20). Jakarta, Indonesia: Lembaga Kesenian Sulawesi Selatan dan Badan Kesenian Indonesia DKI Jakarta.

Ahimzah, H.S. (2007). *Patron klien di Sulawesi Selatan*. Yogyakarta, Indonesia: Kepel.

Bourdieu, P. (1977). *Outline of theory of practice*. Cambridge, England: Cambridge University Press.

Errington, S. (1989). *Meaning and power in Southeast Asian realm*. New Jersey, US: Princeton University Press.

Idrus, N.I. (2005). Siri, gender, and sexuality among the Bugis in South Sulawesi. *Jurnal Antropologi Indonesia*, 29(1), 38–55. Retrieved from http://journal.ui.ac.id/index.php/jai/article/view/3527/2803.

Mattulada. (1985). *Latoa: Suatu lukisan analitis terhadap antropologi politik orang Bugis*. Yogyakarta, Indonesia: Gadjah Mada University Press.

Mattulada. (1998). *Sejarah, masyarakat dan kebudayaan Sulawesi Selatan*. Makasar, Indonesia: Hasanuddin University Press.

Millar, S. (2009). *Perkawinan Bugis*. Makasar, Indonesia: Ininnawa.

Miswar, D., & Setiadi, D. (2010). *Badik titipan ayah*. Jakarta, Indonesia: Citra Sinema SCTV.

Moors, A. (1995). *Women, property and Islam: Palestinian experiences, 1920–1990*. Cambridge, England: Cambridge University Press.

Rahim, R. (2012). *Nilai-nilai utama kebudayaan Bugis*. Yogyakarta, Indonesia: Ombak.

Robinson, K. (2001). Gender, Islam and culture. In K. Robinson (Ed.), *Love, sex and power: Women in Southeast Asia* (pp. 17–30). Clayton, Australia: Monash Asia Institute.

Said, N. (2002). *Tanah sebagai mahar perkawinan*. Depok, Indonesia: Universitas Indonesia.

Yani, A.A. (2007). Budaya politik orang Bugis dalam dinamika. *Jurnal Masyarakat dan Budaya*, 9(2), 105–122.

Court Decisions

Makassar Religious Court Decision No. 210/Pdt.G/2011/PA.Mks, 2011

Makassar High Religious Court Decision No. 080/Pdt.G.2013/PTA-Mks

Makassar Religious Court Decision No. 1575/Pdt.G/2011/PA-Mks

Makassar Religious Court Decision No. 0390/Pdt/G/2011/PA-Mks

PART 2

Women's Visions and Strategies

∵

CHAPTER 3

The Rights of Children Born out of Wedlock

Views of Muslim Women's Organizations on Constitutional Court Judgement 46/2010

Tutik Hamidah

Recent years have seen enormous changes, as well as ongoing debates, regarding the legal status of children born to an unmarried mother. In the countries of the European Union, for example, all children are supposed to have the same civil status regardless of whether their parents were married. This ruling was morally grounded in the idea that all children have human rights claims to equal status and equal access to property. It also was more socially acceptable in that past decades have seen a decline in marriage rates and a rise in ideas of equal rights for people of varied sexual orientations.

The same tendency can be found in Indonesia as well. In this chapter I look in detail at the range of reactions by religiously committed Muslims to a Constitutional Court ruling that recognized the legal status of unmarried fathers with respect to their children. In December 2017, the same court refused a proposal to criminalize sex outside of marriage. Reactions to these and other decisions give us a good understanding of the development, and the diversity of social expectations regarding sex and marriage.

Now to the decision to be analyzed here. Constitutional Court Judgement No. 46/PUU-VIII/2010, issued on 17 February 2012, was ground breaking for Islamic family law in Indonesia. Prior to this, under Marriage Law No. 1/1974 Article 43 (1), children 'born out of wedlock' (*anak luar nikah*) only had a civil law relationship with their mother and their mother's family. Following this judgement, such children were also granted a civil law relationship with their father and his family. This civil law relationship covers family and property relationships in the form of maintenance (payments to cover the cost of living for the child) and inheritance.

The judgement triggered controversy among public figures and civil society organizations. The chair of the Indonesian Commission for Children Protection (Komisi Perlindungan Anak Indonesia, KPAI) and the chair of the National Commission on Violence against Women (Komisi Nasional Anti-kekerasan Perempuan, Komnas Perempuan) were amongst those who supported the

© KONINKLIJKE BRILL NV, LEIDEN, 2019 | DOI:10.1163/9789004386297_005

judgement (Hak anak, 2012).[1] Islamic social organizations in general and the Indonesian Council of Ulama (Majelis Ulama Indonesia, MUI) in particular, protested against it.[2] Although the matter relates directly to women issues, few women expressed their opinions or comments in mass media. Therefore, research was conducted into the views of female leaders of the Islamic women organizations of Muslimat NU[3] and Aisyiyah[4] in the city of Malang, East Java. These two organizations were selected because their boards are comprised of educated women, including wives of Islamic teachers, academics, and judges. Their views reveal mixed support for children born to unofficially wed parents, either religiously wed without legal registration, or not wed at all. This chapter explores Constitutional Court Judgement 46/2010, which treated the rights of such children, as well as the views of Malang female activists on this subject.

Marriage Legitimacy versus Marriage Registration and the Status of Illegitimate Children

According to Indonesian Marriage Law No. 1/1974 Article 2 (1), 'a marriage is legal if it is conducted according to the laws of each person's religion or faith'; Article 2 (2) states that 'every marriage should be registered in accordance with the prevailing legislation'. However, the *Islamic Law Compilation* (*Kompilasi*

---

1 The chair of Indonesia's Commission for the Protection of Children, Aris Merdeka Sirait, expressed appreciation for the Constitutional Court judgement, consulted online on 10 November 2012 https://news.detik.com/jawabarat/1884006/hak-anak-terabaikan-akibat-status -di-luar-nikah and http://www.indopos.co.id/index.php/berita-utama/41-banner-berita -utama/1879-telantarkan-anak-luar-nikah-penjara-mengancam; see also the Komnas Perempuan's statement on the judgement concerning Article 43 (1) of the 1974 Marriage Law, consulted online on 10 November 2012 https://www.republika.co.id/berita/nasional/hukum/12/02/25/lzxre5-komnas-perempuan-sambut-gembira-keputusan-mk-soal-anak-luar-nikah.

2 The chair of the Nahdlatul Ulama Executive Board (Pengurus Besar Nahdlatul Ulama, PBNU), K.H. Sahal Mahfudh, instructed the committee of the NU National Council of Learned Scholars in 2012 to review the limits of citizens' obedience to government in relation to the judgement, which was deemed to conflict with Islamic *shari'a*, consulted online on 3 April 2012 http://www.hasilbahtsu.com/2012/05/putusan-mk-anak-di-luar-nikah.html; K.H. Ma'ruf Amin, chair of the MUI Fatwa Commission, declared that the judgement was excessive, opened the door to adultery, and was destructive of the Islamic legal order, consulted online on 3 April 2012 https://news.detik.com/berita/1866192/mui-nilai-keputusan-mk-soal-status -anak-di-luar-nikah-overdosis.

3 A Muslim organization for women, related to the traditional Muslim organization Nahdlatul Ulama, commonly abbreviated as NU.

4 A Muslim organization for young women related to the modernist reformist Muslim organization Muhammadiyah.

Hukum Islam, KHI) focuses only on the first of these two, thereby sanctioning marriages conducted according to *shari'a* law but not registered with the Indonesian state.[5] According to Article 5 of the KHI, 'a marriage is legal if it is conducted according to Islamic law, under Article 2 (1) of Marriage Law No. 1/1974'. Article 14 of the KHI goes on to state that a marriage is legitimate provided the five pillars of marriage are present: a husband, a wife, a marriage guardian (*wali*) for the wife, two witnesses, and the *ijab kabul* or marriage contract. Thus the presence of the five pillars is sufficient to legitimize the marriage for Muslims under the KHI, without any need to register the marriage with the state. The requirement to register a marriage under Article 2 (2) of the state's marriage law is seemingly negated for Muslims by Article 14 of the Islamic law. This gap between marriage legitimacy and marriage registration affects the status of children, namely the recognition of their parental lineage and claims to maintenance, custody, and inheritance, as well as their mother's rights to joint property and inheritance. This is not an easy problem to resolve because it reflects a contestation of norms in Indonesia's pluralistic society, in this case between the Islamic religious norms and the state's legal norms.

John R. Bowen (2003) argues that Indonesia is a perfect laboratory to study how a pluralistic society struggles with competing norms, which vie to become the basis of its social life (p. 5). This problem, however, is not unique to Indonesia only. Judith E. Tucker (2003) states that other Muslim countries that have reformed their family law, such as Algeria, Egypt, Iraq, Jordan, Kuwait, and Lebanon, emphasize marriage registration as the procedure for legal recognition (p. 71). In another country such as Indonesia, marriages should be registered in order to be legitimate. In Egypt, unregistered marriages are acknowledged but not offered legal protection. In some other countries such as Malaysia, Brunei, and Tunisia, unregistered marriages are sanctioned. The diverse status of marriage registration in Muslim countries indicates that there is a problem related to Islamic marriage law. Writing about Malaysia, Hashim (2014) queries whether registering a marriage legitimizes one that is not legal under Islamic law, and conversely, does not registering a marriage that is legal under Islamic law make it illegal (p. 4)? Unlike Indonesia, Malaysian law does sanction

---

5 Compilation of Islamic Law (KHI) is a corpus of Islamic family law which covers the areas of marriage, inheritance and donation, written in the form of 229 articles as legislation for Muslims in Indonesia. Although the KHI has not yet been incorporated into the official legislation, it has effectively become a guideline to the religious courts based on Inpres No. 1 year 1991 wherein the President instructed the Ministry of Religious Affairs to socialize KHI to use government agencies and communities who need it.

unregistered marriages (Hashim, 2014).[6] Many unregistered marriages exist in Indonesia, where there are no such sanctions. Kate O'Shaughnessy (2009) states that secret marriages in the reform era may be increasing in number, and they are a frequent topic in the print media, academic discussions, and public discourse in general (p. 180).

Bowen (2003) has written in detail of the debates over the legalization of marriage under Marriage Law No. 1/1974 and the ambiguity in the articles that govern the legalization of marriage in Indonesia (p. 183). He has analyzed several court judgements, the judges' views, and also the views of religious figures and female activists to understand the impact of unregistered marriages, often called 'siri' marriages[7] on the status of the wife and the children. Should the husband die and there is no marriage certificate, his wife and children cannot receive a pension from his employer, access his bank account, or claim inheritance (Bowen, 2003, p. 244). Similarly, if the marriage is not registered, there is no *akte nikah* (marriage certificate), and so the religious courts do not recognize it. Mark Cammack and colleagues (1966) suggest that the practice of allowing religion to legitimize marriages paired with the state requirement to have marriages registered was ineffective (p. 64). According to their survey conducted in Indonesia, the religious legitimacy of a marriage and its social recognition were considered more important than state recognition. State recognition was considered only important when there were problems requiring state regulation, such as claims over property and the status of inheritors (Cammack et al., 1966, p. 64).

According to Bowen (2003) there is an ambiguous space between paragraphs (1) and (2) of Article 2, which has given rise to much debate over whether an unregistered marriage should be considered illegal and whether a religious ceremony is sufficient to legitimize a marriage. He argues that this ambiguity was a deliberate decision by the parliamentary factions in the 1970s due to the heated contestation between legal and Islamic norms. Since then, Constitutional Court Judgement 46/2010, which was handed down in 2012, has provided clarification on marriage legality, registration, and the property rights of children born to unregistered marriages. Does this judgment resolve the ambiguity?

---

6 See also Malaysia's Marriage Law, Islamic Family Law Federal Territories Law (IFLFTA) 1984 section 25, 34, 40 and other related articles.

7 *Siri* marriages are done based on the way of religious teachings, without being registered at the government office. Such marriages are sometimes celebrated by inviting large families and neighbors and sometimes in secret.

The Background to Constitutional Court Judgement 46/2010

In 1993 Machica Mochtar married Minister Drs.[8] Moerdiono, the Indonesian secretary of state (1988–1998).[9] Moerdiono was already married at the time and because civil servants were not allowed to have more than one marriage, they married in secret, thus could not register the marriage. A son, Muhammad Iqbal Ramadlan, was born to them. In 1998, the couple divorced[10] and Moerdiono thereafter refused to acknowledge the marriage as his son. Because it was a *siri* marriage, Machica had no legal grounds to sue for recognition of her marriage or her child's status, or any rights to maintenance for herself and her son. She took her case to the Religious Court, the KPAI,[11] and to the women's advocacy group Komnas Perempuan, and, finally in 2008, she applied to the Constitutional Court for a judicial review.[12]

Despite being legitimate under *shari'a* law, Machica's marriage to Moerdiono was considered illegitimate by the state, thus her son's status was also illegitimate. Neither she nor her son were legally considered to have any civil law relationship with Moerdiono, nor did her son have rights to inherit from his father. Mochtar applied for a judicial review on the grounds that Article 2 (2) and Article 43 (1) of the Marriage Law 1/1974 were detrimental to the basic rights of herself and her son.[13] She argued that these two articles invalidated: her rights to form a family and to procreate through a legal marriage; her son's rights for protection from violence and discrimination; both of their rights for

---

8   Drs. was a degree for undergraduates in Indonesia from 1960 to through the 1990s.

9   On 20 December 1993 a wedding took place between Machica Mochtar and Drs Moerdiono, with a now deceased *wali* and now deceased witnesses, with a set of prayer equipment, and 2,000 real and gold and diamond jewellery as *mahr*. See Constitutional Court Judgement 46/PUU-VIII/2010, dated February 17, 2012, concerning a judicial review of Article 2 (2) and Article 43 (1) of the Marriage Law, p. 3.

10   In a siri marriage, divorce is done based on the religious way, with the husband saying the word '*talak*' (I divorced) to his wife, without any trial process.

11   Mochtar complained to the KPAI that her ex-husband's actions had contravened Child Protection Act No. 23/ 2002 and complained to Komnas Perempuan that her ex-husband had committed acts of domestic violence that violated the Eradication of Domestic Violence Law No. 23/ 2004.

12   Machica Mochtar, *Machica Struggled 8 Years for Son's Rights*, consulted online on 1 July 2013 http://selebriti.kapanlagi.com/indonesia/m/machica_mochtar/; http://video .kapanlagi.com/hot-news/machicamochtar-8-tahunberjuang-demi-hakanak.html.

13   As noted earlier, Article 2 (1) of Marriage Law 1/1974 states 'a marriage is legitimate if it is conducted according to the religious law of each religion or faith', while Article 2 (2) states that 'each marriage is registered according to applicable laws'. Article 43 (1) states 'children born out of wedlock only have a civil law relationship with their mother and their mother's family'.

recognition, security, protection, and the certainty of just law; plus their right to equal treatment before the law, as stated in the 1945 Constitution of the Republic of Indonesia.[14]

Nine Constitutional Court judges examined this case, eight Muslims and one Catholic. Some of the judges came from a *pesantren* (traditional Islamic boarding school) background including Chief Justice Mohammad Mahfud. Both the government[15] and parliamentary representatives[16] made submissions in the Constitutional Court hearings on this matter. Constitutional Court Judgement 46/2010 can be summarised as follows:

1. Article 2 (2) of Marriage Act 1/1974 was considered not to be in conflict with the 1945 Constitution. The court explained that: (i) marriage registration is not the determining factor of legitimacy of a marriage, and (ii) marriage registration is an obligation imposed by legislation. Hence it follows that, although unregistered marriages remain legitimate, they do not fulfil administrative requirements and therefore cannot be afforded legal protection. Thus Article 2 (1) and (2) remain in force and were not revised. The court's reasoning was in keeping with those of the government and parliament as presented at the hearing.

2. The wording of Article 43 (1) of Marriage Law 1/1974 was revised as follows: 'Article 43 (1) of Law No. 1/1974 concerning Marriage (Republic of Indonesia 1974 State Number 1, Addendum Number 3019) that states, "A child born out of wedlock only has a civil law relationship with its mother and its mother's family", is not legally binding if it is interpreted to invalidate the civil law relationship with the man, who can be proved by science and technology and/or other legal evidence, to actually have a blood relationship as the child's father, thus this paragraph **must be read as**, "A child born out of wedlock has a civil law relationship with its mother and its mother's family, as well as with the man who is his/her father as can be proven by science and technology and/or other legal evidence to have a blood relationship [with them], including a civil law relationship with their father's family".

---

14 The 1945 Constitution of the Republic of Indonesia, Article 28 B (1) states, 'every person has the right to form a family and have offspring through a legitimate marriage'; Article 28 B (2) states, 'every child has the right to survive, grow and develop and has the right of protection from violence and discrimination'; and Article 28 D (1) states, 'every person has the right to recognition, security, the protection and certainty of just law, and to be treated equally before the law'.

15 Constitutional Court Judgement, 46/PUU-VIII/2010, 14–23.

16 Constitutional Court Judgement, 46/PUU-VIII/2010, 24–29.

THE RIGHTS OF CHILDREN BORN OUT OF WEDLOCK 53

Through this decision, all children, no matter how they are conceived, are considered to have a civil law relationship with their mother and their mother's family as well as with their biological father and his family, provided it can be proven that they have a blood relationship with the father. This second point is opposed to the government and parliamentary submissions that were presented in the Constitutional Court hearing, which stated that, in their view, Article 43 (1) did not discriminate against children but rather protected recognition of their matrilineal descent from their mother, when, as no legitimate marriage existed, their patrilineal descent from their father could not be clearly proven.[17]

Constitutional Court Judge Maria Farida Indriyati issued a concurring opinion, based on different reasoning, stating that if a marriage conducted according to *shari'a* or in secret is considered legitimate by law, thus the children born of these marriages must also be considered to be legitimate. Thus, according to Indriyati, the reference in Article 43 (1) in the 1974 Marriage Law to children born out of wedlock does not refer to children born in a secret or unregistered marriage but children born as a result of adultery, namely children born outside of marriage altogether'.[18] This view suggests that the ambiguous meaning of 'children born out of wedlock' in Marriage Law 1/1974 results from the lack of clarity regarding the status of marriage registration.

The Constitutional Court's judgement triggered a wave of controversy amongst prominent figures in Indonesian society. The term 'children born out of wedlock', as stated in the concurring opinion by Judge Farida, gave the impression of covering children born of secret marriages or outside of marriage, namely children born of adultery. For this reason the Indonesian Ulama Council (MUI) and Islamic social organizations such as the Nahdlatul Ulama (NU) rejected the judgement, declaring that the Constitutional Court judgement had legalized adultery.[19] One month after Constitutional Court Judgement 46/2010 was issued, MUI published a fatwa stating that children born of adultery only have a lineage relationship with their mother, not with their biological father. However their father is obliged to provide maintenance and inheritance through the mechanism of an obligatory will. Point 2 of MUI Fatwa No. 11/ 2012, dated 10 March 2012 concerning 'The status of children born of adultery and their treatment' reads:

---

17   Constitutional Court Judgement, 46/PUU-VIII/2010,14–23.
18   Constitutional Court Judgement, 46/PUU-VIII/2010, 44–45.
19   M. Akbar, *MUI: MK itu seperti tuhan selain Allah*, ed. Didi Purwadi, consulted online on 30 April 2014 http://www.republika.co.id/berita/dunia-islam/islam-nusantara/12/03/20/m16gu6-mui-mk-itu-seperti-tuhan-selain-allah.

1. Children born of adultery have no patrilineal relationship, marriage custody, inheritance, or maintenance ties with their biological father.
2. Children born of adultery only have matrilineal relationship, inheritance, and maintenance links with their mother and their mother's family.
3. Children born of adultery do not bear the sin of adultery committed by their biological parents.
4. *Hadd* sanctions are imposed on adulterers by the authorities in the interests of protecting the legitimate descendants [*hifzh al-nasl*].
5. The government is authorised to impose a *ta'zir* punishment on any male adulterer who fathers a child, obliging him to:
   a. meet the living costs of the child;
   b. provide property after his death through a *wasiat wajibah* [obligatory bequest].
6. The sanction referred in item 5 is intended to protect the children, not to legitimize the children's patrilineal relationship with their biological father.

However, supporters of human rights and children's constitutional rights, such as the Indonesian Children's Protection Commission and the Women's National Commission for Violence against Women, applauded the judgement and declared it to be a 'spectacular breakthrough' in meeting the rights of children born out of wedlock (Telantarkan anak, 2013).[20]

Following Constitutional Court Judgement 46/2010, the Supreme Court issued Supreme Court Circular (SEMA) No. 7/2012 and the Ministry for Domestic Affairs issued an amendment to Population Administration Law No. 23/ 2006. SEMA 7/2012, as explained by Ridwan Mansyur,[21] the Supreme Court's public relations officer, stipulated that children born out of wedlock through *siri* marriages, including *mut'ah* marriages,[22] are entitled to maintenance and a share of their biological father's inheritance through a *wasiat wajibah* (obligatory bequest). He explained that this stipulation is based on the Hanafi *mazhab*, one

---

20 Telantarkan Anak Luar Nikah, Penjara Mengancam. https://www.jpnn .com/news/telantarkan-anak-luar-nikah-penjara-mengancam; http://www.hukumonline .com/berita/baca/lt4f633ebb2ec36/pro-kontra-status-anak-luar-kawin consulted online on 4 July 2013.

21 Religious Court Judges Asked to Consider Children's Rights. Supreme Court hopes the results of this national workshop will be followed up by religious judges all over Indonesia, accessed on July 4 2013, Online, Available at http://www.hukumonline.com/berita/baca/ lt50ba3111c2e10/hakim-agama-diminta-.

22 A *mut'ah* marriage is a marriage for a set time span, for example a month or a week, often referred to as a contract marriage. According to most Sunni ulama, it is forbidden (*haram*) but according to Syiah ulama it is neither forbidden nor recommended (*mubah*).

THE RIGHTS OF CHILDREN BORN OUT OF WEDLOCK 55

of the four schools of thought concerning the interpretation of Islamic law, in which children of adultery are entitled to receive maintenance from their biological father and his family. In the event of the death of the biological father and his biological family, a child born of adultery is also entitled to receive a share of the *wasiat wajibah*, with the amount to be determined by the religious court. Further, with regard to maintenance, fathers must fulfil this duty to avoid being penalised under the Child Protection Law and the Domestic Violence Law.[23]

As for determining the father of a child born out of wedlock, continued the Court, a child has the right to file an application for recognition of their legitimacy to the religious court. This is because children have the right to know for certain who their parents are. The process involves submitting evidence to clarify that the child was born to parents who had a *siri* marriage. The religious court judge will then determine the status of the child. The Supreme Court held meetings with the *KPAI*, USAID, and the Supreme Court Renewal Team to find ways to assist people who lacked the means to obtain legal aid in court, such as by offering help in marriage legalization, wedding certificate and divorce certificate proceedings, and obtaining birth certificates.[24]

Prior to the publication of Constitutional Court Judgement 46/2010, the children of *siri* marriages were only recorded in a side note on the marriage certificate.[25] After the judgement, according to Minister for Domestic Affairs Gamawan Fauzi, because of an amendment of Population Administration Law No. 23/2006, a child born of a *siri* marriage would obtain a child legitimization certificate.[26] Table 3.1 summarises these changes.

The Response of Muslimat NU and Aisyiyah

From the above discussion, it may be concluded that Constitutional Court Judgement 46/2010 is a blessing for children born of unregistered marriages, be they *siri* marriages or *mut'ah* contract marriages. Prior to the judgement, such children were the sole responsibility of their mother, because they did not have

---

23   http://www.jpnn.com/read/2013/02/05/157005/Telantarkan-Anak-Luar-Nikah,-Penjara -Mengancam- Consulted online on 30 April 2014.

24   http://www.padangekspres.co.id/?news=berita&id=40167 Biological Fathers Obliged to Pay Living Costs. Consulted online on 30 April 2014.

25   Before Constitutional Court Judgment 46/2010 children of *siri* marriages could be recorded on the marriage certificate but the only parent listed was his mother.

26   https://nasional.kompas.com/read/2013/12/09/1337569/Mendagri.Anak.dari.Pernikahan .Siri.Bisa.Dapatkan.Akta.Lahir. Consulted online on 30 April 2014.

TABLE 3.1   The status of children born out of wedlock before and after revision

Before revision	After revision	After Constitutional Court's Judgement	
		SEMA 7/2010	Population Administration Law No. 23/2006
Article 43 (1) Marriage Law 1/1974: 'A child born out of wedlock only has a civil law relationship with the mother and the mother's family'.	Article 43 (1) Marriage Law 1/1974: 'A child born out of wedlock has a civil law relationship with the mother and the mother's family and with the man proven by science and technology or other legal evidence to have a blood relationship, which includes a civil law relationship with the father's family'.	(i) A child born out of wedlock (in a *siri* marriage or *mut'ah* marriage) is entitled to maintenance and to receive a portion of the biological father's inheritance through a *wasiyat wajibah*. (ii) If the biological father does not fulfil his obligations, he may be penalized under the Child Protection Law and the Protection Against Domestic Violence Act. (iii) A child born out of wedlock is entitled to request a legitimization-legitimization certificate from the religious court, by presenting the evidence of the parents' *siri* marriage.	A child born of a *siri* marriage will obtain a legitimization certificate.

a civil law relationship with their biological father. This state of affairs, according to the National Commission against Violence against Women, was a form of discrimination against women.[27] Women bear multiple burdens, namely social stigma and the sole responsibility for paying for the children's upkeep and education. Before the judgement, an irresponsible father could walk away and not be legally liable. For this reason, Constitutional Court Judgement 46/2010 could also be described as a blessing for women.

The Muslimat NU and Aisyiyah are the two largest Islamic women's organizations in Indonesia. Both have intensive women's advocacy programs and various activities. The Muslimat NU has a varied *da'wah* (preaching) program and women's groups that attract participants from the highest levels of society to the grassroots. These groups include *jama'ah tahlil* groups, which gather to

---

27   'Komnas Perempuan Sambut Gembira Keputusan MK Soal Anak Luar Nikah' (National Commission of Women welcomes the Constitutional Court's decision on illegitimate children), *Republika*. Consulted online on 2 November 2017, http://nasional.republika.co.id/berita/nasional/hukum/12/02/25/lzxre5-komnas-perempuan-sambut-gembira-keputusan-mk-soal-anak-luar-nikah.

THE RIGHTS OF CHILDREN BORN OUT OF WEDLOCK 57

chant verses of the Koran, and are led by a leader in the community; *diba'an* groups, which also engage in chanting and praising Muhammad; *khotmil* Qur'an groups, which read the Koran from cover to cover; *manaqib* groups, which praise Syekh Abdul Qadir Jailani, a respected Sufi leader; and *istighosah* groups, which gather to pray for particular needs.[28] They also provide kindergarten and health services through the Mother and Child Health Clinic (Balai Kesehatan Ibu dan Anak), and lately they have also been intensely involved in the activities of their women's crisis centre. Aisyiyah has a similar number of programs, namely women-only gatherings for religious learning (*majelis taklim*), kindergarten, and health and integrated clinics[29] for women.

The programs offered by Muslimat NU and Aisyiyah suggest that the two organizations and the leaders who run them well understand women's issues and concerns. The board members of these organizations are highly educated, and their members include respected female *pesantren* (wives/daughters of Muslim clerics), *muballighat* or female preachers, judges, and parliamentarians. Thus, these boards were viewed as competent to respond to Constitutional Court Judgement 46/2010. Six informants were selected, three from each organization. Mirroring some of the controversial reactions to the judgement, and protests from MUI in particular, the informants' responses were divided according to the type of marriage: they found the judgement to be a good development for children born of *siri* marriages, but less so for children born of adultery.

Responses to Changes in the Status and Rights of Children Born of *Siri* Marriages

Female leaders of the Islamic women's organizations Muslimat NU and Aisyiyah found that children born of *siri* marriage are most benefited by Constitutional Court Judgement No. 46/PUU-VIII/2010. Nyai Hajah Chasinah, first chair of Muslimat NU and a *muballigh* from a traditional *pesantren* religious educational background, said:

> I agree 100 per cent with the Constitutional Court Judgement, if what is meant by 'children born out of wedlock' refers to children born of *siri* marriages. Children born of *siri* marriages are legitimate offspring according

---

28 These groups routinely meet once a week, once every two weeks, or once a month. At the end of their sessions there is a talk about morals, worship, and contemporary issues.

29 These offer integrated services, health, happy family coaching, protection from domestic violence. and family planning services.

to religion so they have the same rights as children of registered marriages. Because if they are not treated in this way, then children born as a result of adultery could also just be included as legitimate offsprings. So, this Constitutional Court Judgement is still open to multiple interpretations. There are many views, some support it and others less so, if the interpretation of 'children born out of wedlock' is not children born of *siri* marriages, but children born of any marriage whatsoever.[30]

Chasinah clearly differentiates between children born of *siri* marriages and children born of adultery, arguing that children born of *siri* marriages have the same rights as children born of registered marriages, because *siri* marriages are legitimate according to religion. This view fits with the general idea mentioned earlier that marriage is a religious duty and that the legitimacy or illegitimacy of a marriage is based on religion. For this reason, Chasinah agrees with the Constitutional Court Judgement that a patrilineal relationship should be acknowledged for children born of *siri* marriages, but not for children born of adultery.

Siti Aminah, a Muslimat NU advisor and former member of the Malang District Parliament stated:

> I strongly agree, the intellectual groups have made a breakthrough in protecting the children born of *siri* marriages. They must be given the same rights as legitimate children from registered marriages. *Siri* marriages are allowed, according to Islam, they are legitimate; one feels sorry for the woman, and the party who suffers is the woman. *Siri* marriages are allowed in order to give marriage legitimacy. For instance, nowadays young people go out with each other, the boy wants to conduct a *siri* marriage to legitimize the relationship. But they should quickly follow it up with a registered marriage. However, if the *siri* marriage is instead an excuse for a second or a third wife, I disagree. For a polygamous relationship, the second marriage must be a formal marriage. A child from a *siri* marriage has a patrilineal descent from their father, but to act as a guardian the father does not have any formal documents supporting that. Now the government has provided a child legitimization certificate, so, yes, that is a very good solution.[31]

---

30 Interview in the Pelangi Hotel, 14 October 2013.

31 Interview at Pelangi Hotel, 14 October 2013.

THE RIGHTS OF CHILDREN BORN OUT OF WEDLOCK

Aminah's response echoes Chasinah's: the lineage status and the rights of children born in *siri* marriages are the same as those of children born in registered marriages, because, although *siri* marriages are not acknowledged by the state, they are legitimate according to religion. Aminah added that, although *siri* marriages are *halal*, she did not agree with *siri* marriages being used for polygamy purpose because she felt sorry for the wives. Polygamous unregistered marriages, according to Aminah, often end in divorce, after children are already born. Such marriages cause suffering for the women because there is no marriage certificate. While the judgement does not address this problem, it has at least somewhat overcome the problem of the children's status. For this reason, Aminah strongly agrees with the judgement.

Hajah Sulalah is a member of the Muslimat NU's research and development institute and a lecturer in the Tarbiyah (Education) Faculty in the Maliki State Islamic University (UIN/Universitas Islam Negeri) in Malang. Her response was the same as Chasinah and Aminah's:

> The lineage and the rights of a child are to the father, because the child was born after the marriage contract was made, even though it is a *siri* marriage according to the state. It is the state that defines the marriage as *siri*. So I agree with the Constitutional Court's judgement, and consider it a solution for children born of a *siri* marriage. I agree with *siri* marriage because the fact is, it remains legitimate according to *shari'a*, and we cannot oppose this when there areproper grounds and conditions. For example, there are cases where young couples get together and spend all their time together and do things like that, and it is better that they get married in a *siri* marriage and, once they finish their studies, have the marriage registered. According to religion that is positive, a good thing, but it will still be a problem. And the woman also, if the man asks to have sex, it is a sin for the woman to refuse because she is already his wife. But when they have sex and then have children, they cannot register their children. So yes the Constitutional Court Judgement is the solution that children born in *siri* marriages have been waiting for.[32]

According to Sulalah, parents usually marry off their children in *siri* weddings to avoid the sin of their children for committing sex before marriage. Young people who are still attending university, are not yet prepared to raise a family, might have a *siri* marriage to avoid the sin of premarital relations.

---

32   Interview in Pelangi Hotel, 14 October 2013.

Hajah Rukmini, chair of Aisyiyah and professional *muballigh*, also agreed with the others, and added that the legitimacy of *siri* marriages was ultimately a matter of the piety of the couples marrying: 'If people have faith in the Day of Reckoning, even though [the marriage] is not registered, they will be accountable. So *siri* marriages are an issue of the faith of each couple involved'.[33] Hajah Sukanah, a member of Aisyiyah and a former judge of the religious court, also agreed with the others. As a former religious court judge, she understood how complicated *siri* marriages were, as they related to children, joint property, and inherited property when the husband passed away. According to Sukanah, prior to the judgement, any problems were settled through the kindness of the first wife: 'With polygamous marriages, the first wife determines the children's fate. Because of that, this judgement of the Constitutional Court is very helpful'.[34]

Komariah, chair of Aisyiyah's Law and Human Rights Council, and a lecturer in the Faculty of Law at the Muhammadiyah University in Malang, declared:

> If someone thinks that the rights and responsibilities in a *siri* marriage will be the same as legally registered marriages at the Religious Affairs Office, particularly for women, clearly this is incorrect. Because the marriage is not registered in any state office, obviously women will not receive what they wish, such as maintenance, inheritance etc., in contrast to when they were formally married. However, with the issuing of Constitutional Court Judgement 46/2010 followed by SEMA 7/2010 as well as the amendment to Population Administration Law 23/2006, the status and the rights of children now have legal protection. I think it is positive because the children are blameless.[35]

Komariah's response was like those of the others, namely positive, provided the term 'children born out of wedlock' referred to children born in *siri* marriages. In cases of adultery, the women also found the children to be blameless, but agreed with religious law that they should not be entitled to all of the provisions that children of *siri* marriages receive.

---

33 Interview in Rukmini's home, 17 October 2013.
34 Interview in the Malang Muhammadiyah Office, 18 October 2013.
35 Interview in Pelangi Hotel, 14 October 2013.

Responses to the Changes in the Rights and Status of Children Born of Adultery

Logically, a child born of adultery also belongs to the definition of 'illegitimate child' in the Constitutional Court Judgement No. 46/PUU-VIII/2010. Therefore, he should also get the blessing of the verdict, but the MUI refuses to grant the child of adultery the same status and rights as the child of *siri* marriage. I asked the female leaders of the Islamic women's organizations Muslimat NU and Aisyiyah about this distinction.

Chasinah's response matched her *pesantren* educational background, which is strongly oriented towards Islamic law. When asked about how she felt about the judgement in relation to children born of adultery, she declared:

> If a woman commits adultery and becomes pregnant, well, there are stipulations concerning a child before three months in the womb. In the Qur'an, there are stipulations regarding lineage, livelihood, and marriage partners. Two stipulations stand out. Firstly, when a woman marries a man with whom she committed adultery before the third month of her pregnancy, then the child's lineage is to the father. Secondly, if she marries him after three months of pregnancy then Islam would consider her to be not pregnant and thus no *iddah* [waiting period for marrying] is required. However, [with regard to this case] the MUI provided a fatwa to protect the children, obliging the biological father to provide maintenance and inheritance when he dies. I consider this to be a humane gesture, which we owe them, because the children have done no wrong, they must not be punished, and as the MUI fatwa states they must not be ostracized. So, I strongly agree.[36]

As Chasinah's statement makes clear, for children born of adultery, the time of their mother's marriage determines whether their patrilineal status is recognized or not. If the mother marries before her pregnancy is three months old then the child's relationship with the father is recognized, but not after that point, even if the father is proven by a DNA test.

Aminah also agreed with the MUI fatwa, stating:

> As for children born of adultery, this is a difficult issue. I think the government should make a special regulation, or maybe the MUI fatwa may

---

36   Interview in Pelangi Hotel, 14 October 2013.

be implemented. The biological father is asked to take responsibility for the provision of maintenance, and a *wasiyat wajibah* if he dies instead of inheritance, but the child cannot declare patrilineal lineage and the father cannot be the child's guardian at the child's wedding. I agree if it is stipulated like the MUI fatwa.[37]

Sulalah agreed with the judgement, and wanted to see further action, stating:

> In my opinion, the Constitutional Court Judgment is correct: in any case, a biological father of a child must take responsibility for his actions. So basically, I support the decision of the Constitutional Court, as I want to focus on one aspect of the child that they are born pure, and from another aspect we see that a person (including an infant) must not be punished for their parents' behaviour. I see that a child born of adultery receives much pressure, from social, moral, economic and other aspects. So, seeing the conditions of the children who are unjustly disadvantaged by this act of adultery, I would strongly agree that we should present a recommendation that the government publish an Anti-Adultery Act, and not wait too long for that.[38]

Sulalah's response differs from Chasinah and Aminah's and could be described as liberal, as she crosses the literal stipulations of the hadith. According to Sulalah, as long as a blood relationship can be determined, through a DNA test for example, a child has the same rights as a child born in a legitimate marriage. Her argument is that Islam considers every child to be born in a condition of purity (*fitrah*); there is no original sin in Islam. According to the hadith the lineage recognized of a child born of adultery is from his mother, but in those days, there was no scientific proof to determine the father of a child born of an adulterous woman. The principal law is that a child's lineage is from his father and mother, unless the father rejects it. Sulalah agrees that such children should be provided full rights, including the rights to lineage, guardianship, and inheritance, provided a blood relationship is proven.

According to Rukmini and Sukanah, humane considerations must be balanced against religious stipulations. Rukmini stated:

---

37   Interview in Pelangi Hotel, 14 October 2013.
38   Interview in Pelangi Hotel, 14 October 2013.

THE RIGHTS OF CHILDREN BORN OUT OF WEDLOCK 63

Concerning children born of adultery, I agree with the MUI, namely that the responsibilities of the biological father remain, but the religious rights, such as guardianship and other rights, these must be questioned. However, their right to inheritance – they did get a chance there through the *wasiyat wajibah*, didn't they? In law, there is 'what the law intends to achieve' [the *maqasidus syariah*] and there is the 'wisdom of the law' [the *hikmatut tasyri*].[39]

Similarly, Sukanah said:

The lineage of a child born of adultery remains with the mother, yes, and the child receives no rights, the father cannot be a guardian, the child's guardian in the marriage is by the judge and the child receives no inheritance. This is clear if the child is born of adultery. Even when fatherhood is proven through a DNA test, the law remains, the child has no rights according to religion.[40]

Komariah essentially agreed with the provision of rights to a child born of adultery, both from the perspectives of the Constitutional Court judgement and from the MUI fatwa, and she chose to highlight the challenges of implementation. Komariah focused on the implementation of the judgement:

I strongly agree with the Constitutional Court Judgement as well as the MUI fatwa, in which there are two philosophical principles, the first being the protection of the children and the second the punishment of the perpetrators.

And how about the position of the children? Related to the legal vacuum concerning the meaning of the civil law relationship, the minimum provision is the *nafkah hadhonah* [daily maintenance] and *wasiyat wajibah*. The only issue concerns with how to realize the facts in court. Judges understand this well. To actually provide maintenance for the children and to realize this are very difficult.[41]

As a judge, Komariah knew that the provision of maintenance for legitimate children following divorce is already an intricate matter. Provision of mainte-

---

39   Interview in Rukmini's home, 17 October 2013.
40   Interview in Muhammadiyah office, 18 October 2013.
41   Interview in Pelangi Hotel, 14 October 2013.

nance for children born of a *siri* marriage or adultery is even more problematic in the implementation. Komariah felt that the government need to pay more attention to the implementation of this issue and to provide more supports to the courts in settling these matters.

Conclusion

The rights of 'children born out of wedlock' underwent a revolutionary change along with Constitutional Court Judgement 46/2010. The leaders of Muslimat NU and Aisyiyah were unified in their positive responses to the provision of rights to children of *siri* marriages. In their responses, they asserted that *siri* marriage is legitimate according to religion; and that the rights and obligations that emerge from a *siri* marriage should not differ from those of registered marriages. Hence the children of a *siri* marriage should have the rights of lineage, provision of living expenses, guardianship, and inheritance, just as do the children in a legitimate registered marriage.

However, the leaders of Muslimat NU and Aisyiyah seemed to disapprove of *siri* marriages, especially when this type of marriages were often used to commit polygamy. They repeatedly warned the dangers of *siri* marriages to their community, namely the women's *majelis taklim*. In their views, *siri* marriages could be tolerated if parents wanted to prevent their children from committing sins in premarital relations, in condition that their children will later be officially married and registered.

From these responses of the leaders of Muslimat NU and Aisyiyah, we may conclude as follows. Firstly, Constitutional Court Judgement 46/2010 is a long-awaited solution to the problems experienced by children born of *siri* marriages. Secondly, classical Islamic law is strongly dominant in their interpretation of Islam. Not only do the leaders of Muslimat NU, who generally have a *pesantren* educational background, but also do Aisyiyah leaders, who generally have formal, non-traditional Islamic educational backgrounds, presented classical Islamic law arguments. Thirdly, they all strongly agreed with the importance of marriage registration, even though registration is not a religious requirement of a marriage. This was based on their awareness of the importance of having legal protection.

In addition, there were two views expressed on the rights of children born of adultery. The majority agreed with the provision of maintenance and inheritance under a *wasiyat wajibah* for the children, based on humanity reasons, but they did not support the recognition of lineage ties or guardianship, or inheritance rights for children born of adultery. The argument was based on

THE RIGHTS OF CHILDREN BORN OUT OF WEDLOCK   65

the MUI fatwa.[42] The others (in the minority) agreed to the provision of lineage, maintenance, guardianship, and inheritance rights to the children of adultery, provided the biological father acknowledges the child. They argued that, in principle, a child's lineage is from the father and mother, unless the father rejects it. The hadith that declares a child of adultery has lineage ties only with the mother should be understood in its historical context, not literally.

These findings show that leaders of the Islamic women's organizations such as Muslimat NU and Aisiyah strongly believe in following the opinions of the scholars (*ulama*) especially if the scholars of NU, Muhammadiyah and MUI have agreed. Most of the leaders think that the legal phrase 'children born out of wedlock' should be taken as referring to children who are products of *siri* marriage, not adultery, even if paternity can be tested by DNA test. Therefore, they think that the MUI's fatwa is more acceptable than the Constitutional Court Judgement 46/2010, although they feel it is inhumane for children for not being able to claim lineage to their biological father as well as for the mother who has to sustain full parental responsibility and suffers from social stigma. According to these findings, it may be concluded that the renewal of the law is more acceptable as long as it is in line with the agreement of the majority of Indonesian scholars, *ulama*, but also that opinions of these scholars can change. We can expect to see further debates and conflicts about the relations among state marriage, sexualities, and the status of children, all are strongly shaped by both shifting social norms and *ulama* judgements.

Bibliography

Akbar, M. (2012). MUI: MK itu Seperti 'Tuhan Selain Allah'. *Republika*. Retrieved from http://www.republika.co.id/berita/dunia-islam/islam-nusantara/12/03/20/m16gu6 -mui-mk-itu-seperti-tuhan-selain-allah, consulted online on 30 April 2014

Anwar, Samsul MH & Munawar, I.M.H. (2012). *Nasab anak di luar perkawinan paska Putusan Mahkamah Konstitusi Nomor 46/PUU-VIII/2010 tanggal 17 Februari 2012 menurut teori fikih dan perundang-undangan*. Retrieved from http://www.badilag.net/ data/ARTIKEL/ARTIKEL%20NASAB%20ANAK%20DI%20LUAR %20PERKAWINAN.pdf, consulted online on 8 April 2014

Al-Zuhaily & Wahbah. (1985). *Fiqh al-Islam wa Adillatuhu*, Juz VII. Damaskus: Dar al-Fikr.

---

42   See MUI Fatwa No. 11/2012 concerning The Position of Children Born of Adultery and Their Treatment.

Ayah Biologis. (2013). Ayah Biologis Wajib Memberikan Biaya Hidup. *Padang Ekpres.* Retrieved from http://www.padangekspres.co.id/?news=berita&id=40167 on 30 April 2014

Bowen, J.R. (2003). *Islam, law and equality.* New York, NY: Cambridge University Press.

Cammack, M., Young, L.A., & Heaton, T. (1966). Legislating social change in an Islamic society: Indonesia's marriage law. *The American Journal of Comparative Law, 44* (1), 45–73.

Chairullah, E. (2013). Anak hasil nikah siri dapat akta kelahiran. *Kemendagri.* Retrieved from https://nasional.kompas.com/read/2013/12/09/1337569/Mendagri.Anak.dari .Pernikahan.Siri.Bisa.Dapatkan.Akta.Lahir. Consulted online on 30 April 2014.

Hak Anak. (2012). Hak anak terabaikan akibat status di luar nikah. *Detiknews.* Retrieved from https://news.detik.com/jawabarat/1884006/hak-anak-terabaikan-akibat -status-di-luar-nikah consulted online on 10 November 2012

Hakim Agama. (2012). Hakim Agama diminta perhatikan hak-hak anak. *Hukum Online.* Retrieved from http://www.hukumonline.com/berita/baca/lt50ba3111c2e10/hakim -agama-diminta-, consulted online on 4 July 2013

Hashim, N.M. (2009). *Non-registration of Muslim marriages in Malaysia: Socio-legal implications.* Paper presented at the International Conference on Law and Social Obligations: Law and social obligations: The way forward obligations, 10–11 August, Faculty of Law, University of Kashmir, Srinigar, India. Retrieved from http://irep.iium .edu.my/3353/.

Komnas PA. (2012). Komnas PA: 249 anak kasus perceraian tak diakui ayahnya. *Republika.* Retrieved from http://www.republika.co.id/berita/nasional/umum/12/04/03/ m1w2c3-komnas-pa-249-anak-kasus-perceraian-tak-diakui-ayahnya, consulted online on 4 April 2012

Komnas Perempuan. (2012). Pernyataan Sikap Komnas Perempuan terhadap Putusan Mahkamah Konstitusi tentang Pasal 43 Ayat 1 UU No. 1/1974 tentang perkawinan. *Komnas Perempuan.* Retrieved from http://www.komnasperempuan.or.id/2012/02/ pernyataan-sikap-komnas-perempuan-terhadap-putusan-mahkamah-konstitusi -tentang-pasal-43-ayat-1-uu-no-1-tahun-1974-tentang-perkawinan/

Kontroversi. (2012). Kontroversi putusan MK tentang anak di luar nikah. Retrieved from http://lbm.lirboyo.net/kontroversi-putusan-mk-tentang-anak-di-luar-nikah/ consulted online on 3 April 2012

Machica. (2012). Machica struggled for 8 years for her son's rights. *Kapanlagi.com.* Retrieved from: http://video.kapanlagi.com/hot-news/machicamochtar-8 -tahunberjuang-demi-hakanak.html,consulted online on 3 April 2012

MK dituding. (2012). MK dituding legalkan zina. *Joglosemar.* Retrieved from http://revisi .joglosemar.co/berita/mk-dituding-legalkan-zina-67643.html, consulted online on 4 April 2012

MUI Nilai. (2012). MUI nilai keputusan MK soal status anak di luar nikah overdosis. Detiknews. Retrieved from https://news.detik.com/berita/d-1866192/mui-nilai-keputusan-mk-soal-status-anak-di-luar-nikah-overdosis, consulted online on 2 April 2012

Mukti, A. (2012). Diskusi hukum Putusan Mahkamah Konstitusi RI Nomor 46/PUU-VIII/2010. Retrieved from http://badilag.net/data/ARTIKEL/DISKUSI%20HUKUM.pdf, consulted online on 8 April 2012

O'Shaughnessy, K. (2009). *Gender, state and social power in contemporary Indonesia*. New York, NY: Routledge.

Pro Kontra. (2012). Pro kontra status anak luar kawin. *Hukum Online*. Retrieved from http://www.hukumonline.com/berita/baca/lt4f633ebb2ec36/pro-kontra-status-anak-luar-kawin, consulted online on 2 April 2012

Puslitbang, K. (2012). There are still no legal sanctions to crimes in marriage. Retrieved from http://puslitbang1,balitbangdiklat.kemenag.go.id/index.php?option=c, consulted online on 1 April 2012

Purnomo, I.W.A. (2012). Ayah bertanggungjawab atas anak di luar nikah. Retrieved from http://www.tempo.co/read/news/2012/02/17/063384763/MK-Ayah-Bertanggung-Jawab-atas-Anak-di-Luar-Nikah, consulted online on 2 April 2012

Purwadi, D. (2012). MUI: MK itu seperti 'Tuhan Selain Allah'. *Republika*. Retrieved from http://www.republika.co.id/berita/dunia-islam/islam-nusantara/12/03/20/m16gu6-mui-mk-itu-seperti-tuhan-selain-allah, consulted online on 2 April 2012

Putusan MK. (2013). Putusan MK tentang Anak di Luar Nikah. *Indonesia Today*. Consulted online on 3 July 2013. http://www.itoday.co.id/politik/putusan-mk-tentang-anak-di-luar-nikah-legalkan-zina

Safitri, A.R. (2012). Komnas Perempuan sambut gembira Keputusan MK Soal Anak Luar Nikah. *Republika*. http://nasional.republika.co.id/berita/nasional/hukum/12/02/25/lzxre5-komnas-perempuan-sambut-gembira-keputusan-mk-soal-anak-luar-nikah Consulted online on 2 November 2017

Salmande, A. (2013). Ketua MUI ibaratkan MK seperti tuhan. *Hukum Online*. Retrieved from http://www.hukumonline.com/berita/baca/lt4f68c6f92726d/ketua-mui-ibaratkan-mk-seperti-tuhan, consulted online on 8 April 2013

Tucker, J.E. (2003). *Women, family and gender in Islamic law*. New York, NY: Cambridge University Press.

Telantarkan Anak. (2012). Telantarkan anak luar nikah, penjara mengancam. *Indo Pos*. Retrieved from http://www.indopos.co.id/index.php/berita-utama/41-banner-berita-utama/1879-telantarkan-anak-luar-nikah-penjara-mengancam, consulted online on 10 November 2012

Telantarkan Anak. (2013). Telantarkan anak luar nikah, penjara mengancam. *JPNN*. Retrieved from https://www.jpnn.com/news/telantarkan-anak-luar-nikah-penjara-mengancam, consulted online on 4 July 2013

Law and Legislation

Constitutional Court Judgement, 46/PUU-VIII/2010

Fatwa MUI No. 11/ 2012 dated 10 March 2012 on The Position of Children Born out of Adultery and Their Treatment

Islamic Family Law Federal Territories Law (IFLFTA) 1984

Presidential Instructions No. 1 of 1991 on Compilation of Islamic Law

Judgement of the Constitutional Court of the Republic of Indonesia No. 46/PUU-VIII/2010 dated 27 February 2012

Indonesian Constitution of 1945

Law No. 23 of 2002 on the Protection of Children

Law No. 1 of 1974 on Marriage and the Compilation of Islamic Law

CHAPTER 4

Inheritance for Women

The Role of Lawyers in Women's Access and Rights

Nanda Amalia

Inheritance may be a crucial social and emotional issue in many communities, as inheritance disputes place heirs in a tense situation. This issue is even more critical when inheritance law is implemented in a society with a strong patriarchal culture that places women in a subordinate position. Inheritance can be viewed as either a given, something that is pre-determined by religion and customary law, or a matter where equity must be sought for weaker members of the community.

The issue of inheritance itself occupies a special position in studies of family law, covering studies on marriage law, custody law, and the division of joint property (Otto, 2009 Lev, 1962, 1990, 1996a, 1996b). Scholars have studied many different legal actors involved in inheritance: legislative institutions, police, judiciaries, lawyers, and others in the legal profession. In many anthropological studies actors are analyzed through cultural frameworks in which their actions are seen as the result of socially prescribed behavioural guidelines. Studies on the role of lawyers in a setting of legal pluralism are, however, somewhat rare.

This chapter uses a methodology of socio-legal studies to examine the role of lawyers in cases involving women's inheritance in Aceh, a setting distinguished by the presence of *shari'a* courts with a new degree of authority over various legal matters. Acehnese society's resistance to the national legal system has resulted in various new legal formulations (Miller, 2008; Robinson, 1998). The resulting legal pluralism means that inheritance cases may be settled through mediation at the village level or through a legal process in the *shari'a* (religious) or district (state) court. Cases may then proceed to further arbitration at the High Court or the Supreme Court. Three cases involving women being represented by lawyers and having their cases heard in the *shari'a* court and/or district court are presented here.

This research was driven by my desire to build an understanding of gender issues from a socio-legal studies perspective and to critically analyze how women are positioned in the implementation of justice with respect to inheritance disputes. The contestation and representation of male-female relations in the legal system reveal how power works. In this chapter, I look at cases

© KONINKLIJKE BRILL NV, LEIDEN, 2019 | DOI:10.1163/9789004386297_006

where power is vested in the person of the lawyer as an actor defending the rights of their client or their own interests, and one who has a deep understanding of not only the case materials but also the position of the plaintiff in a complex legal arena with shifting centres of power.

In these cases, although each party involved in litigation has prepared their suits based on various legal or *adat* (customary law) norms, it is the lawyer who plays a definitive role in the settlement. The lawyer as a legal actor, highly skilled in various legal manoeuvres and relations, is of particular importance in understanding material outcomes in cases brought by women, and especially in the province of Aceh, whose special legal status as the sole province where the legislature may pass laws based on *shari'a* makes the issues of gender equity and the authority of the national legal system come under near-constant negotiation (Lev, 1965, 1996; Wieringa, 2006). How do lawyers intervene, what are *their* interests, and how do they shape outcomes?

Inheritance for Women

Women's legal status is often problematic in Muslim countries or in Muslim communities where *shari'a* law is implemented (Wieringa, 2009; Sandberg & Hofri-Winogradow, 2010; Robinson & Bessel, 2002; Robinson, 2004, 2008; Peletz, 2002; Lindsey, 2008, p. 195; Lev, 1972; Koeswadji, 1976, p. 339; Holike, 2011, 71; Ghassemi, 2009; Basu, 2005; Bahramitash, 2004). Many studies have revealed the marginalised position of women in the public sphere (Siapno, 2002; Ichwan, 2013, p. 137; Idria, 2013, p. 180; Nur & Inayatillah, 2011). Islamic inheritance law is based on the Qur'anic verse An Nisa 11, which states that all biological children, be they male or female, are the heirs of their deceased parents. A preliminary study conducted by Daniel S. Lev (1990) raises multiple questions concerning the position of the widow as heir, as this is laid out in state law (p. 11). Is she also recognized as the heir of her deceased husband? If not, then what rights does she have over the estate to support herself in the future? Lev's study sought to explain the impact of developments in the thoughts of Supreme Court justices on the issue of inheritance in Indonesian customary law. Lev writes that most inheritance law in Indonesia does not identify women as heirs, and that this is the norm in societies that follow a patrilineal inheritance system, such as in Tapanuli in North Sumatra, Bali, and Lombok. In some places, women have responded by creating their own legal subculture, for example, Sulistyowati Irianto (2003) describes how women in the Toba Batak society select judicial institutions for settling inheritance disputes.

Erman Rajagukguk's (2009) study of Sasak (Lombok) society analyzes the inheritance-related struggles of women and society in general in a pluralistic legal context, and maps three approaches to inheritance. In the first approach, adopted by a small proportion of the community who closely follows customary law, women do not receive any inheritance rights. In the second approach, people take inheritance disputes to the religious court, which follows Islamic law as well as the Supreme Court jurisprudence that divides inheritance in a 2:1 (male: female heir) proportion. Rajagukguk comments that this seems to be the concern of the Supreme Court, which takes a very careful stance when it comes to the provisions of the Qur'an and hadith. The third approach is taken by some Muslim Sasaks who present their cases to the district court. In the cases Rajagukguk studied, the district court divided the inheritance equally between the male and female children in one decision, on the grounds that there have been social changes concerning the position of women in Lombok society.

John R. Bowen (2005) argues that pre-existing social norms are the main grounds for judges' legal reasoning in Indonesia. How men and women work together in the rice fields and share the burden as well as the fruits of their labour are taken as evidence of equality and justice. In line with Bowen, Ratno Lukito (2006) states that 'gender neutral inheritance is one of the most complicated problems faced by the state in the issue of varied inheritance practice' (p. 147). Based on the two cases analyzed in his study, Lukito concludes that the Supreme Court believes in the principle of equality and justice for all heirs, without taking into account gender identity, and uses this as the basis for settlement of inheritance disputes. A more recent study conducted by Mukhtar Zamzami (2011) argues that inheritance law emphasizes non-discriminatory principles or the principle of gender equality. This principle is open, in a way that if heirs agree on other divisions of property, albeit unequal ones, these also may be accepted.

However, practices do not always follow this principle. For Aceh, IDLO case study reports (2006), Fitzpatrick (2008), and Harper (2010) agree on the weak position of women in regards to inheritance and land rights. This condition occurs due to the weak understanding of law in society, which is aggravated by the existence of erroneous interpretations among some people of the provisions of Islamic law that regulate inherited property. The study finds that women often face injustice because their husbands or brothers dominate property ownership. In many cases, women's relatives – 'her mother, sisters, and other female relatives' – do not obtain their due inheritance from their biological child or blood brothers because, according to customary law and the community's views, they are not entitled to receive inheritance, especially if the deceased husband has a male sibling or a cousin. These studies demonstrate that, in practice, inheritance laws (both formal law and customary law) are not rigidly implemented. How an inheritance is divided is very much determined by the decisions of the customary law elders, agreements between the children of the deceased, and the economic status of the deceased and the domicile.

With regard to these conditions – and particularly with regard to the vulnerability of women who lack knowledge of the law, have no bargaining power within society, and have no access to obtain their rights – it must be asked: who are the legal actors who can forge a way for them to get their share of inheritance? Several studies show that judges in the religious courts have contributed to women's position in court proceedings, for example, Arskal Salim and colleagues (2009) document the paradigmatic and behavioural shift amongst judges in Aceh and South Sulawesi, who have developed sensitivity towards the issue of equality of women's and men's rights following training. However, the degree of sensitivity amongst individual judges varies, and must be developed. One way to do this is through *ijtihad* (legal reasoning), as demonstrated by Akhmad Khisni (2011) in a study of the Republic of Indonesia's Supreme Court Decision No. 86 K/AG/194, dated 28 April 1995. The judges ruled that the daughter should receive the total share of the property left by the deceased, reasoning that the existence of a living son or a daughter extinguished the inheritance rights of the deceased's blood relatives, except for the parents or spouse. This decision established a legal principle that the meaning of the words 'walad' (son) and 'aulad' (children) cover both male and female children.

In addition to judges, government officials at the *kampong* or village level can also play a role. In Aceh various regulations, including Regional Regulation Number 7/2002 concerning the Implementation of Customary Law Life, authorise customary law institutions to resolve certain social issues such as inheritance. This is similar to what occurs in Sasak society, where some inheritance cases can be resolved by government bureaucracy at the village level (Rajagukguk, 2009). However, in several cases decided by the religious court, lawyers provided background information to raise women's awareness of their equal inheritance rights before the law. Sadly, Rajagukguk has not yet conducted an in-depth exploration of the impact of the presence of these lawyers and their legal information sessions, particularly for women in inheritance cases.

One of the most complete current studies in this field is that of Lukito (2012), in his article entitled 'The Training, Appointment, and Supervision of Islamic Lawyers in Indonesia', which discusses how professional lawyers perform in the more pluralistic legal fields. The study offers 'a descriptive overview of the training, work and professional regulation of Islamic lawyers in contemporary Indonesia' (Lukito, 2012, p. 65). Lukito's study also provides a comparison of lawyers who practice in the religious courts in Indonesia, Malaysia, and Singapore, but it does not provide further detail on the role of lawyers in handling inheritance cases on behalf of women.

As stated at the beginning of this chapter, the key question for this study is: 'Is inheritance for women a given or is it rather something that must be strived for?' While Islamic law decrees that women are entitled to inheritance, in reality this is not something that tends to happen by itself. Women (wives, daughters, mothers, second wives, wives in a polygamous marriage, wives married in *siri* [Arabic for hidden, secret]) must struggle for their inheritance rights. Do interventions by lawyers help or hinder these struggles?

In the next sections, this chapter explores three inheritance disputes. The first case of inheritance and joint property is a case brought by a wife against her stepchildren.[1] The parties had initially agreed to divide the deceased's estate by family agreement, but because the division was considered unfair by the plaintiff, the second wife of the deceased, on the direction of her family and lawyer this case was brought before the Lhokseumawe *shari'a* court.

The second case concerns an inheritance dispute between a sole daughter and her uncle. On the advice of the Bungong Jeumpa Foundation of Banda Aceh, the daughter chose to attempt to resolve the dispute through mediation at the village level, accompanied by the foundation's staff and lawyers. Attempted settlement of the case at the *gampong* level was considered the appropriate first step of the dispute resolution process.[2]

The third case, a dispute over property rights, was brought before the Lhokseumawe district court by a widow, a first wife, as the plaintiff, with the second wife as the defendant. This case is interesting not only because the dispute was between two wives and their families over their inheritance from their deceased husband but also because, after the plaintiff's lawyer provided counsel, the case was brought before the district court, with a suit for 'payment of losses resulting from actions contrary to the law', instead of being brought before the *shari'a* court as a dispute over the property of the deceased.

In the following sections, I focus on the interactions between the female heirs and their lawyers, as well as the interactions between the lawyers and the judges in court. From a sociological perspective, social interaction is considered a social process that occurs largely through imitation, suggestion, identifica-

---

1   Case Registration No. 65/Pdt.G/2011/Ms-Lsm.
2   Interview with Wanti Maulidar, Director of Bungong Jeumpa Foundation, 29 June 2011.

tion, and sympathy (Soekanto, 2003, pp. 59–67). I argue that, in these three cases, the lawyers were mostly motivated by sympathy to take on the cases, in addition to their belief that the state should guarantee everyone's constitutional rights for recognition, protection, and equal treatment before the law.[3]

Lawyer–Client Interaction in an Inheritance and Joint Property Dispute between a Second Wife and Her Stepchildren

This first case was a joint property dispute between Nona (a pseudonym), the second wife of the deceased, and the children of the first wife, initially filed in the Lhokseumawe *shari'a* court in 2011. The *shari'a* court decision, Number 65/Pdt.G/2011/Ms-Lsm, was appealed to the Aceh High Court before a final decision was handed down from the Supreme Court. The disputed property was valued at just under 20 billion rupiah in the form of various goods and assets. This case was quite complex due to the following factors: (1) the value of the estate under dispute, (2) the fact that the site of each real estate item was controlled by the defendant, (3) the relatively lengthy settlement period,[4] (4) the challenge to the legal standing of the plaintiff's marriage to the deceased,[5] (5) the resentment of the defendants over the presence of the plaintiff in the household of their deceased father and their biological mother, and lastly (6) the presence of legal counsels for both parties.[6]

---

3 Further, see Law No. 16/2011, concerning Legal Aid.

4 This case was filed on 18 March 2011, and the Supreme Court handed down an appeal (*kasasi*) decision after this study was completed in 2013. In 2013, parties were still participating in mediation sessions, each party accompanied by a lawyer (interview with the plaintiff's legal counsel, on 12 January 2013).

5 As the marriage between the plaintiff and the deceased was considered invalid by formal law, the defendants appealed that 'The plaintiff's suite is baseless and lacks legal grounds because there was no legal relationship between the plaintiff and the defendants'. In their view the plaintiff was not an heir to their deceased father, because the plaintiff had not been legally married according to the provisions of Law No. 1/1974, and even the wedding certificate provided as evidence in this case they considered to be fake. This was because the wedding of the plaintiff and her husband (the defendants' father) took place in 1990, when the plaintiff's husband was still bound in legal marriage to the mother of the defendants and had not sought permission from the religious court to marry a second wife. The deceased did not divorce his first wife until 2000.

6 In the city of Lhokseumawe, it is relatively rare for legal counsels to assist a case. Judge Fitriel Hanif (interview on 28 September 2011) considered this to be an interesting case, made more interesting by the presence of the legal counsel. The presence of experienced legal counsels was felt by the judges to somewhat ease their burden in court proceedings.

INHERITANCE FOR WOMEN

I was unable to directly access, meet, or interview either the plaintiff and defendant parties as they were away during the period I was conducting research. The parties' lawyers were also reluctant to facilitate meetings with their clients for various reasons. However, comprehensive opportunities were provided to interview each lawyer, both when the case was proceeding at court as well as outside the court schedule. The summary of the case thus relies on the information provided by the parties' legal counsel.

Munir (a pseudonym), Nona's lawyer, became involved in the case on the recommendation of a friend of the plaintiff. The lawyer was authorised to handle this case following preliminary communication and consultation between them. In the lawyer's view, it was important for him to assist Nona because he felt she completely lacked any knowledge on matters of the law and he was concerned that she would not be able to exercise her rights without his legal assistance. To illustrate his point, he related that during one of the mediation processes Nona had agreed to share a plot of land and a building with her stepchildren, which belonged to her and her deceased husband according to the property deed. The lawyer stated:

> When the lady just agreed to share her property, it was as if she was just surrendering to fate, although when we investigated the land and the shop that her stepchildren were giving her [in return], we found that they were unproductive assets. Meanwhile they were taking over the rest of the property amounting to around 16 billion rupiah and we understand that the deceased's businesses are still operating and one of the businesses is working on a contract with Perusahaan Listrik Negara (PLN)—the state electricity company.[7]

However the defendants' lawyer Zahara (a pseudonym)[8] believed that the plaintiff's lawyer had deliberately delayed the settlement of the case, and suspected he was no longer prioritising his client's interests. In fact, once during the mediation process in the *shari'a* court, the mediating judge asked the plaintiff's lawyer to leave the room, and then questioned the plaintiff who answered, 'I want an amicable settlement but I don't know how to tell that to my lawyer'.[9]

---

7   Interview with Judge Fitriel Hanif on 28 September 2011.

8   Zahara is a female lawyer in a Jakarta-based law firm. Her presence as legal counsel in this case began at the request of relatives of the defendants, who happened to be close neighbours of Zahara's family.

9   Interview with Zahara, on 5 February 2012.

Below I consider the different claims presented by the parties, their complaints, and the responses of each party to the complaints. Each party appeared adamant they should have full control of the property left by the deceased husband and father.[10] The plaintiff claimed she was entitled as the deceased's wife to a share of their joint property as well as the inherited property. Meanwhile, the defendants submitted that they were the ones rightfully entitled to the estate, as the plaintiff lacked any rights due to the unregistered nature of her marriage to the deceased.[11]

The responses that arose and how the parties tried to construct the existing facts seemed to be very contrary to each other, and this was influenced by the attorneys' recommendations and direction. Initially after the deceased passed away, the plaintiff and defendants agreed to settle the inheritance division through deliberations at the village level. However, once the plaintiff's lawyer arrived, the situation developed into a dispute that was brought to the court. There the plaintiff argued that the property division suggested by the defendants was not a fair treatment of the plaintiff's rights as second wife. The case was filed with the court of first instance, the Mahkamah Syaríyah in Lhokseumawe, and continued at the appeals level at the Aceh Syari'yah High Court as well as the appeal process to the Supreme Court. The judges of this tribunal rendered their verdict and declared the lawsuit unacceptable (*Niet Ontvankelijke Verklaard*), with consideration that there were insufficient parties in the case (*Plurium litis consortium*), as the first wife was not involved as a party to the case. The judges reasoned this was because the rights to the joint property under dispute were possessed by the plaintiff, the plaintiff's husband, and the first wife.

When I last spoke to lawyer Munir in 2013,[12] each party was considering returning to mediation. It was not clear if the lawyers would still assist the case

---

10   The assets that were the objects of dispute consisted of 27 items, including a house, a shop and house, land, cash, lands with fish/prawn ponds, four four-wheeled vehicles, one six-wheeled vehicle, stock for sale in an electrical shop, gold, savings in several banks in Lhokseumawe, as well as insurance.

11   Privately Zahara admitted that the defendants knew about the marriage of Nona and their deceased father, but because the marriage took place when the deceased and their mother had not yet legally divorced in the religious court and no permit for polygamy had been granted by the first wife, the defendants objected to sharing the assets. Further, during the hearing, the marriage certificate presented by Nona was revealed to be false. Interestingly, as a lawyer providing legal aid, Zahara stated that as a woman she was most concerned at the cases of injustice befalling women, but not, she emphasised, 'for women as second wives'.

12   Interview with Munir in Lhokseumawe, 11 January 2013.

INHERITANCE FOR WOMEN

and at what stage or level mediation would be conducted, whether internally within the family or before the customary law institution in the village or even at the *shari'a* court.

Joint Property Dispute between a Sole Daughter and Her Uncle

In several inherited property cases in Aceh, daughters have had their inheritance rights marginalised. My interview with a female judge[13] in the Aceh High Court confirmed this. She described an inheritance dispute between two daughters and their uncle that was appealed at the Aceh High Court and decided in favour of the deceased's daughters over the uncle, as the daughters still needed funds to continue their education and support their lives.

When the uncle protested this ruling, the chief of the High Court reviewed the case and reprimanded the panel of judges over the decision. Judge Hafidzoh, one of the panel judges, responded that their decision was based on Supreme Court jurisprudence.[14] She did not appear concerned about the plaintiff's demonstrations or objections. As Bowen (2005) writes, 'equality and fairness are socially appropriate bases for choosing among alternative interpretations of the law' (pp. 191–192). A study conducted by Al Yasa Abubakar (1989) also found that within the framework of rejuvenated *fiqh* in the field of inheritance there have been several significant changes, with one related to the existence of biological offspring. The study concluded that whilst there were still direct living relatives, indirectly related kin were not entitled to inheritance.

This introduction provides some context for a similar case between a young woman, Zamrah (pseudonym), and her uncle in an inheritance dispute over joint property owned by her biological mother and her stepfather. This property was in the form of a plot of land and a house that had been taken over by her uncle Miswardi (pseudonym), who felt he was more entitled to the inheritance than the daughter. The case underwent mediation at the village level as discussed below.

Zamrah was assisted by the Bungong Jeumpa Foundation (Yayasan Bungong Jeumpa, YBJ),[15] a non-governmental organization focussed on client support

---

13   Interview with Masdarwiati, 9 July 2011.

14   See also Republic of Indonesia Supreme Court Decision No. 86 K/AG/194, dated 28 April 1995.

15   YBJ was founded in August 2005 by a group of friends who had previously been involved in NGOs in Aceh working on post-tsunami issues. YBJ received funding from the Aceh Reha-

programs in inheritance cases. The information presented below was obtained through a study of the files related to this case, testimonial video documentation of the handling of the case from Zamrah and others, as well as an interview with the director of YBJ and paralegal assistants.

This dispute began in 2007 with the daughter's visit to YBJ, after hearing a radio broadcast about their work providing information programs about inheritance.[16] The case began after the Aceh tsunami killed Zamrah's biological parents, Zamrah's stepfather, and the children of her mother and stepfather. As the sole remaining child Zamrah felt entitled to a share of her deceased mother's property. However, the land and house that had been rebuilt with the help of the tsunami rehabilitation program was controlled by her uncle.

YBJ's handling of the case began by explaining to Zamrah the Islamic legal provisions concerning inherited property. YBJ paralegals subsequently conducted field investigations where the property in the form of land and a house was located. YBJ, through the Centre for Advocacy Studies in Inheritance Rights (Pusat Studi dan Advokasi Hak Warisan/PSAHW), then requested Zamrah to authorise them to conduct the next steps, namely mediation at the village level and, if required, litigation in the *shari'a* court or the local district court.[17]

The PSAHW's efforts were challenged by the uncle, who was determined to control the property. According to PSAHW paralegals Ridha and Muttarwali,[18] the uncle's refusal was based more on the prevailing social conception that the rights of a sole daughter would be hindered by the existence of an uncle. The inheritance dispute settlement process between them was mediated by PSAHW along with indigenous elders in the village. PSAHW had an equal role as that of the elderly in the village to reconcile the two, especially to defend the interests of Zahara as the heir. Ridha said that the dispute settlement undertaken by Zamrah and her uncle didn't take long, and was solved just in the third meeting. They agreed to equally share the inheritance between the two of them. This agreement was reached after the village elders, especially the ulama, advised on the importance of deliberation in resolving disputes, especially in inheritance cases. The ulama also submitted the basic religious law as stated

---

bilitation and Reconstruction agency Aceh-Nias, Johannitter International, and HIVOS. In 2007 YBJ had two teams, the first working on illiteracy and the second on inheritance.

16 Clearly the radio broadcast was a fascinating and effective promotion of YBJ activities, as evident from this case.

17 Interview with YBJ Director Wanti Maulidar, in Banda Aceh, 24 April 2012. YBJ's handling of the case was confirmed by Ridha Wahyuni Harahap, a YBJ paralegal officer, on 24 April 2012.

18 Interview with Ridha and Muttarwali, in Banda Aceh, 26 April 2012.

INHERITANCE FOR WOMEN

in QS An-Nisa verse 11: one single daughter will receive an inheritance of half of the total inheritance, and the remaining half will be distributed to the other heirs.

This case suggests that the presence of paralegal officers assisted by lawyers in handling inheritance disputes for women has increased the likelihood that women may gain access to their rightful inheritance. It is also reduces the possibility of women's rights being denied under customary law or certain interpretations of Qu'ranic verses.

Property Dispute in the District Court between First and Second Wives

The third case concerns a dispute over property in the Lhokseumawe district court brought by a first wife against a second wife over the estate of their deceased husband. This case was selected to highlight the involvement of lawyers in this case, which, once the dispute was settled through court mediation, left the plaintiff unsatisfied and still disappointed three years after the matter was resolved.

The plaintiff's family decided to employ the services of the male lawyer Effendi to handle this case because they believed that lawyers would have access to the court, understand the law, and understand the legal process. They had already attempted to resolve the matter through mediation via the customary law forum in the village. Nina (a pseudonym), the biological child of the first wife, stated:

> actually, this case had been brought for settlement in the village, where the object of dispute lay, but we felt that the villagers were biased in settling this case, even though the evidence that we presented indicated that the shop-house in dispute was rightfully our mother's to inherit, but with various excuses the village people tended to prioritise the interests of our father's second wife.[19]

---

19 Interview with Nina on 21 January 2013. According to Nina, it was understood that before the deceased passed away, the assets he owned had been divided amongst his two wives and their respective children. The first wife had five children and the second wife had two children. According to Nina the assets in the form of the shop-house was declared by their father to be part of their mother's (the first wife) share, but somehow the ownership deed of the shop-house and land came into the possession of the defendants, the family of the second wife. The deeds were in the name of the deceased.

The end result of this litigation was that an agreement was mediated between the parties through the Lhokseumawe district court, as set out in Mediation Certificate Number 17/Pdt.G/2009/PN-Lsm, Concerning Compensation. Nina stated, 'Though we understand that by law we must comply with the court's decision, actually we are not satisfied. In fact, the true justice we desired could not be fulfilled by the court'. Nina further revealed they were disappointed with the lawyer because they felt 'the lawyer never demonstrated a commitment to the plaintiff from the beginning, despite the plaintiff being the lawyer's client. In fact, the lawyer tended to be money oriented'.

Nina explained that this dispute began shortly after their late father passed away, and it became known that two lands and building ownership titles, which the plaintiff viewed as belonging to their mother, were controlled by the second wife, and the shop and dwelling had already been leased to another party by the defendant.

The first meeting of the plaintiff and the lawyer Effendi was to discuss the plaintiff's position. They came to court well prepared, although the lawyer later admitted to me that there was a possibility they might make a 'deal' with the opposition. Effendi understood that, as the plaintiff's lawyer, they could not also provide legal advice to the defendants directly because of the code of conduct. Thus, Effendi subsequently invited a junior lawyer[20] who also practiced in the Lhokseumawe region to handle and assist this case, in order to benefit not only from his own clients but also from the defendants.

According to Effendi, a junior lawyer was involved because if a senior lawyer were invited it would become impossible to 'share' this case,[21] which invites the question, what caused Effendi to risk taking such a professionally unethical stance? Or was it – as Effendi claimed – motivated by an intention to offer the best solution for both sides: because both parties were heirs, they should not bicker over property but rather receive their due share?

Nina confirmed meeting with the opposition's lawyer in Effendi's law firm office where discussions were also held over the case at hand. Privately Nina was taken aback that there was another party privy to the case Nina was pre-

---

20 The term 'junior lawyer' here is used to differentiate from the senior lawyers that already have their own legal offices and have a high number of work hours.

21 Interview with Effendi, 23 January 2013. The term 'sharing' was used by Effendi to refer to dividing the costs of assisting the case that they could receive from the client (the defendants). He felt that he had the right because the defendants had requested his assistance but because of his position as the plaintiff's lawyer, it was not possible for him to actively assist the defendants.

INHERITANCE FOR WOMEN

senting to court.[22] Nina did not at first question the other lawyer or her own lawyer about what was going on, though she admitted she felt suspicious of her lawyer. She said:

> If I felt *su'udzon*,[23] it would appear that our lawyer had made a deal with the opposition. So maybe the lawyer received one share from us and one or a half from our opposition. So, again I say he is looking for money. Although we did not have it written in black and white, we had already agreed on the lawyer's rights in addition to their fee for representing us and a fee based on the value of the object of dispute.[24]

Nina did at one point directly question her lawyer regarding their commitment to assist them and promise to win the case. But, she said, the lawyer quite skilfully avoided blame and gave an excuse. Nina explained:

> There was no written agreement in the beginning, was there? Because of that, I must say, that being a lawyer is a profession, and a profession means looking for money. So if he thinks that he can make a quick buck, why would he take the slow path such as handling our case up to the appellate or cassation level?[25]

Further, Nina said that, although the parties had indeed not drawn up a contract, at the time the plaintiff as well as all the children and the extended family who made the recommendation were present and witnessed the event.

Effendi told me that his approach was actually a lawyer's 'method' for handling a case. His justification was that the disputed property was still part of the estate, but, because the defendants controlled the ownership certificates, he directed his client to present the case to the district court as a dispute of ownership lawsuit. The plaintiff's party stated they did not understand why this case was being filed at the district court rather than the *shari'a* court but they assumed the lawyer knew better. In settling this case, the lawyer strongly encouraged the plaintiff to take a conciliatory position, which later bothered

---

22 According to Nina at the time of the conversation it appeared that the opposition's lawyer did not know for certain who his client was and even thought that Nina was his client, which caused the lawyer to elaborate his explanation of the possibility of a '*deal*' that their party could obtain through Effendi.

23 *su'udzon* (Arabic), meaning to think ill of someone.

24 Interview with Nina, 21 January 2013.

25 Interview with Nina, 21 January 2013.

the plaintiff. The plaintiff claimed that the lawyer had often urged her and her children to find it in their hearts to relinquish half of the disputed property to the defendants, arguing on religious and moral grounds that the defendant's children were also of the same flesh and blood.

Effendi confirmed that he had indeed provided much direction to the plaintiff and her family, based on the idea of the value of family. His reasoning was that both parties understood the context of the polygamous marriage they had shared with the deceased, and thus he advised them to simply divide the disputed assets 50–50, meaning one shop-house for the plaintiff and another shop-house for the defendant.

Both parties were deeply dissatisfied with the attitude of the lawyer they had chosen. The plaintiff considered the lawyer to be purely profit oriented, seeking profit not only from his own client but also from the defendants, through collaboration with his colleague, the junior lawyer.

Conclusion

Just like judges, lawyers play a large role in enabling women to exercise their rights in inheritance cases in court. Given the marginalised condition of women in Aceh, and their lack of access and awareness of the legal system, the role played by lawyers is needed. However, in two of the three cases explored, female heirs lacked confidence and/or the ability to negotiate with their lawyers. In the first case, the plaintiff appeared anxious and unable to communicate her wishes to the lawyer, and in the third case, the lawyer was not committed to representing the best interests of the plaintiff as initially agreed and the plaintiff lacked a clear understanding of the legal process.

This tendency for lawyers to be motivated by fees and profits has been frequently and widely discussed. Conversations about the idea that 'whoever has more money will be favoured by the law' are no longer confined to criminal cases but are also apparent in private cases. The study by Susan Daicoff (1971) in America provides evidence for this. A significant increase in the number of lawyers has caused competition amongst lawyers, which has caused various crises of professionalism, such as domineering and aggressive attitudes, antagonistic attitudes, the prioritization of material gain, and the selection of only clients capable of paying, leaving clients without means behind. In the lawyer's path to achieve personal success and recognition, such behaviour eventually erodes moral values and undermines their professionalism. Looking at these three cases, we might ask: What brings a lawyer to truly assist an heir?

The customary law system of dispute settlement through mediation, whilst being easier to comprehend and easier to access than the formal judiciary system, can suffer from a lack of neutrality and consistent guidelines. Lawyers may be considered more able to help settle existing disputes, due to their competence, professionalism, and access to formal justice. However, the neutrality the client expects will be challenged should the lawyer insist on following 'their way' and seek to fulfil their own economic interests over their client's interests. Moreover, bringing cases to court, rather than settlement through customary law, has changed the tone of local debates, involving outside parties and eroding feelings of kinship. For women seeking a just share of material assets, the actions of lawyers may offer better access to the machinery of law, but at a risk of bringing in conflicting interests and not effectively understanding – and representing – their clients' interests.

Bibliography

Abubakar, A. (1989). *Ahli waris sepertalian darah: Kajian perbandingan terhadap penalaran Hazairin dan penalaran fiqih mazhab.* (Unpublished doctoral dissertation). Jogjakarta, Indonesia: UIN Sunan Kalijaga.

Bahramitash, R. (2004). Myths and realities of the impact of political Islam on women: Female employment in Indonesia and Iran. *Development in Practice, 14* (4), 508–520.

Basu, S. (2005). *The politics of giving: Dowry and inheritance as feminist issues.* New Delhi, India: Women Unlimited.

Bowen, J.R. (2005). Fairness and law in Indonesian court. In M. Cammack & M. Feener (Eds.), *Islamic law in contemporary Indonesia: Ideas and institutions* (pp. 170–192). Harvard, MA: Harvard University Press.

Daicoff, S. (1971). Lawyer, know thyself: A review of empirical research on attorney attributes bearing on professionalism. *The American University Law Review, 46, 1337–1428*

Fitzpatrick, D. (2008). Women's rights to land and housing in tsunami-affected Aceh, Indonesia. Singapore: National University of Singapore, Asia Research Institute.

Ghassemi, G. (2009). Criminal punishment in Islamic societies: Empirical study of attitudes to criminal sentencing in Iran. *European Journal on Criminal Policy and Research,* 15 (1–2), 159–180.

Harper, E. (2010). *Promoting legal empowerment in the aftermath of disaster: An evaluation of Post-Tsunami Legal Assistance Initiatives in Indonesia.* IDLO Legal Empowerment Working Paper. Legal Empowerment: Practitioners' Perspectives: 157. Rome, Italy: International Development Law Organization.

Holike, C. (2011). The state of Islam: Negotiating democracy, Muslim women's rights and morality in Indonesia and Malaysia. In A. Fleschenberg & C. Derich (Eds.), *Women and politics in Asia: A springboard for democracy?* (pp. 71–95). Singapore: Institute of Southeast Asian Studies.

Ichwan, M.N. (2013). Alternatives to shariatism: Progressive Muslim intellectuals, feminists, queers and sufis in contemporary Aceh. In Kies Van Dijk (Ed), *Regime change, democracy and Islam: The case of Indonesia* (pp. 137–179). Jakarta: Islam Research Program (IRP).

IDLO (International Development Law Organization). (2006). *Guardianship, inheritance and land law in post tsunami Aceh.* Banda Aceh, Indonesia: IDLO.

Idria, R. (2013). Cultural resistance to shariatism in Aceh. In K. van Dijk (Ed.), *Regime change, democracy and Islam: The case of Indonesia* (pp. 180–201). Leiden: Universiteit Leiden.

Irianto, S. (2003). *Women between various choices of law.* Jakarta, Indonesia: Yayasan Obor Indonesia.

Khisni, A. (2011). Independent legal reasoning (ijtihad) of Religious Court judges in the field of Inheritance Law and its contribution to national law. *Jurnal Hukum, 18*, 146–163.

Koeswadji, H.H. (1976). Law and development: The legal status of women in Indonesia, their role and challenge in creating a new national law. *Malaya Law Review, 18* (2), 339–360.

Lev, D.S. (1962). The Supreme Court and adat inheritance law in Indonesia. *The American Journal of Comparative Law, 11* (2), 205–224.

Lev, D.S. (1965). The lady and the Banyan tree: Civil-law change in Indonesia. *The American Journal of Comparative Law, 14* (2), 85–105.

Lev, D.S. (1972). *Islamic courts in Indonesia: A study in the political bases of legal institutions.* Los Angeles, CA: University of California Press.

Lev, D.S. (1987). *Legal aid in Indonesia* (Vol. 44). Clayton, Australia: Monash Asia Institute.

Lev, D.S. (1990). Hukum dan politik di Indonesia: Kesinambungan dan perubahan (pp. 1–32). Jakarta, Indonesia: LP3ES.

Lev, D.S. (1996a). Between state and society: Professional lawyers and reform in Indonesia. In T. Lindsey (Ed.), *Indonesia Law and Society* (pp. 144–163). New York, NY: Cornell University.

Lev, D.S. (1996b). On the other hand? In L.J. Sears (Ed.), *Fantasizing the feminine in Indonesia* (pp. 191–203). Durham, NC: Duke University Press.

Lev, D.S. (1998). Lawyers' causes in Indonesia and Malaysia. In *Cause lawyering: Political commitments and professional responsibilities* (pp. 431–452). New York, NY: Oxford.

Lindsey, T. (2008). When words fail. Syariah law in Indonesia: Revival, reform or transplantation? In *Examining Practice, Interrogating Theory: Comparative Legal Studies in Asia* (pp. 195–222). Leiden. Brill.

INHERITANCE FOR WOMEN 85

Lukito, R. (2006). *The enigma of national law in Indonesia: The Supreme Court's Decisions on Gender-Neutral Inheritance*, pp. 147–167. Retrieved from http://commission-on-legal-pluralism.com/nl/journal_of_legal_pluralism.

Lukito, R. (2012). The training, appointment, and supervision of Islamic lawyers in Indonesia. *Pacific Rim Law and Policy Journal, 21* (1), 65–83.

Miller, M.A. (2008). *Rebellion and reform in Indonesia: Jakarta's security and autonomy policies in Aceh* (Vol. 10). London: Routledge.

Nur, M.R.M., & Inayatillah. (2011). Women's marginalization from public spaces: The case of Aceh. *Asian Women, 27* (4), 55–79.

Otto, J.M. (2009). Islam, family law, and constitutional context in Indonesia. In E. Cotran & M. Lau (Eds.), *Yearbook of Islamic and Middle Eastern Law* (2006–2007) 13, pp. 73–86. Leiden: Brill.

Peletz, M.G. (2002). *Islamic modern: Religious courts and cultural politics in Malaysia.* Princeton, NJ: Princeton University Press.

Rajagukguk, E. (2009). *The pluralism of inheritance law: Case study of women's rights in the island of Lombok, West Nusa Tenggara.* Retrieved from http://www.ermanhukum.com.

Robinson, G. (1998). Rawan is as rawan does: The origins of disorder in New Order Aceh. *Indonesia, 66,* pp. 127–157.

Robinson, K. (2004). Islam, gender, and politics in Indonesia. In Virginia Hooker & Amin Saikal, *Islamic perspectives in the new millennium* (pp. 183–198). Singapore: ISEAS.

Robinson, K. (2008). *Gender, Islam and democracy in Indonesia* (Vol. 6). London: Routledge.

Robinson, K.M., & Bessell, S. (2002). *Women in Indonesia: Gender, equity, and development* (Vol. 8). Singapore: Institute of Southeast Asian Studies.

Salim, A., Nurlaelawati, E., Natsir, L.M. & Sayuti, W. (2009). *Demi keadilan dan kesetaraan: Dokumentasi program sensitivitas gender Hakim Agama.* Jakarta, Indonesia: Puskumham and The Asia Foundation.

Sandberg, H., & Hofri-Winogradow, A. (2010). Arab women's renunciation of their portions of family wealth-reflections in the Civil Courts. *Tel Aviv University Law Review, 33,* 373–385.

Siapno, J.A. (2002). *Gender, Islam, nationalism and the state in Aceh: The paradox of power, co-optation and resistance.* London, England: Routledge Curzon.

Soekanto, S. (2003). *Sosiologi: Suatu pengantar.* Jakarta, Indonesia: Raja Grafindo Persada.

Wieringa, S.E. (2006). Islamization in Indonesia: Women activists' discourses. *Signs, 32* (1), 1–8. doi:10.1086/505274

Wieringa, S.E. (2009). Women resisting creeping Islamic fundamentalism in Indonesia. *Asian Journal of Women's Studies, 15* (4), 30–56.

Zamzami, M. (2011). *Kajian hukum terhadap kedudukan dan hak perempuan dalam sistem hukum kewarisan Indonesia dikaitkan dengan azas keadilan dalam rangka menuju pembangunan hukum kewarisan Islam.* (Unpublished doctoral dissertation). Bandung: Padjajaran University.

PART 3

The Role of Judges

CHAPTER 5

Women's Financial Rights after Divorce in Indonesia

Euis Nurlaelawati

According to the state law, Indonesian women have certain rights upon divorce. Despite those provisions, many women remain in a weak position, and in order to get those rightful provisions enforced, women often have to go to court. Rahmah, Sulastri, and Nur'aeni [pseudonyms] are three women who went to court to demand their rights when their marriages were no longer sustainable. Appearing in the courts of Tangerang and Serang, Rahmah and Sulastri were defendants in their husbands' divorce suits, while Nur'aeni filed her own divorce petition. In court, the women described their marital problems and requested that their post-divorce rights to *iddah* maintenance (payments made to the woman during the waiting period after divorce) and *mut'ah* (gift of consolation) be upheld. These were granted but not to their full satisfaction. Nonetheless, compared to other women with similar cases, they were more fortunate. In fact, most of women I observed involved in custody and child maintenance cases remained in a weak position and unable to claim their rights to these types of support.

The rights of women have long been a central topic in Islamic legal discourse in the Muslim world, including Indonesia (Tucker, 2008; Cammack, 1999; Mir-Hosseini, 2006). A number of Muslim scholars argue that juridical recourse to classical Islamic legal doctrines is one of the barriers preventing Muslim women from achieving equality and justice. In line with reforms to meet the demands of contemporary life, Muslim countries have made legislative changes, which have led to the increased empowerment and improved legal status of women (Hirsch, 1998; Tucker, 2008; Cammack, 1999), including in Indonesia (Nasution, 2002).

These legal reforms were also made to meet the demands of feminist activists for gender equality, a comparatively recent global phenomenon. Some feminists have questioned why, in states that claim to be guided by *shari'a* justice, equality is not well reflected in the laws that regulate gender relations and the rights of men and women. Ziba Mir-Hosseini (2006), for example, has questioned this issue in Iran where, she understands, Muslim jurists and Muslims in general believe that justice and equality are intrinsic values of Islam

© KONINKLIJKE BRILL NV, LEIDEN, 2019 | DOI:10.1163/9789004386297_007

and cardinal principles in *shari'a* law. She observes, however, that movements have emerged to bring legal practices more in line with these principles (Mir-Hosseini 2006, 2013).

Through Marriage Law No. 1/1974, Indonesia introduced a number of legal reforms on familial issues (Soewondo, 1997, pp. 284–285). The Marriage Law, which applies to all Indonesian citizens regardless of their religion, and which serves as a reference for judges of both civil and Islamic religious courts, is the result of a long struggle by Indonesian gender activists and women in general. As I have argued elsewhere, previous divorce and polygamy practices in Indonesia had strongly disadvantaged women. A woman seeking divorce had to file a petition in court, while a man could merely visit the Kantor Urusan Agama (Office of Religious Affairs, KUA) to formally finalize the divorce by making a unilateral declaration before his wife (Nakamura, 1983). The 1974 Marriage Law provided a number of reforms, including giving women equal access to divorce (Bowen, 2003; Cammuck et al., 2007, pp. 112–114) and with easier procedures (Sumner & Lindsey, 2010). Polygamy has been restricted to those husbands who can meet certain requirements. These provisions were also adopted in the *Kompilasi Hukum Islam* (Compilation of Islamic Laws), subsequently referred to as the *Kompilasi*, which applies only to Muslims.

Women's post-divorce rights were increased by the 1974 Marriage Law and the *Kompilasi*. Generally, under these Indonesian Islamic legal provisions, after divorce women have the right to custody of the children, *iddah* maintenance, child support, and a gift of consolation (*mut'ah*). While women's rights to custody and child support exist in all cases of divorce, *iddah* maintenance and *mut'ah* are only granted to the woman if the divorce petition is filed by the man. If divorce is filed by the woman (*khuluk* divorce) with monetary compensation, women are less likely to receive *iddah* maintenance and *mut'ah*.

A number of works have discussed various aspects of women's post-divorce rights in Indonesia, including Salim and colleagues (2009), Bowen (2003), and van Huis (2011). Salim and colleagues look at the gender sensitivity of judges and examine a number of cases to see how judges use their knowledge of gender and equality in resolving cases. They find that judges with more knowledge of gender equality tend to favour women with regard to their post-divorce rights. Bowen scrutinizes how various norms have influenced judicial discretion on the issue of gender equality. In his study of the implementation of *iddah* maintenance in Cianjur court, van Huis discusses the attitude of husbands concerning their obligation to pay and how wives attempted to obtain their rightful settlement in court.

My previous study, a report for the Islam Research Program, which was based on a research conducted in 2013 (Nurlaelawati, 2015), examined the legal position of women and children in general legal practice, and demonstrated that women now have better access to justice in some cases but remain in a weak position in other cases. In polygamy and custody cases, women mostly remain in a subordinate position as they often lack the power to argue against their husband's authority or decision to marry again. However, almost all the petitions filed by women in court were approved and women have felt more positive about courts since 2009, when their treatment by the courts improved. Pro bono advocacy programs, the circuit court, and the Centers for Legal Aid (Pos Bantuan Hukum) have led women to feel more positive about courts (Nurlaelawati, 2013). With regard to *iddah* maintenance, I found that women have been better protected by judges. Judges now require husbands to agree to a set amount of money for payments of *iddah* maintenance, *mut'ah*, and child support. However, have these judges' attempts enabled women to fully obtain their rightful payments? And how do women present their demands?

In this chapter I focus on the provisions and practices, including *iddah* maintenance, *mut'ah*, and financial support for children, that comprise women's rightful financial support, and on court judgments and their legal reasoning. Through examining a number of cases, I also demonstrate how women negotiate their rights to property, state their demands, and fight for justice, a struggle whose success is not without challenges. This chapter is based on data gathered from two methods of research, bibliographical and empirical investigations, through interviews, observations of hearings, and analysis of decisions. Conducted in two courts, empirical research included interviewing 23 female litigants and 10 judges, and attending 28 hearings, 16 in the Tangerang religious court and 12 in the Serang religious court, of divorce cases filed by either husbands or wives. Of these, nine divorces were filed by husbands, six of them in the Tangerang Religious Court, and three in the Serang Religious Court, and nineteen divorces were filed by wives, ten of them in the Tangerang Religious Court and nine in the Serang Religious Court. Thirty-six divorce case decisions were collected from the Serang religious court and another 36 decisions from the Tangerang Religious Court, all issued between 2007–2009, with 18 cases filed by husbands and 18 by wives in each court. My discussion is based on the data that I gathered from these documents and that I obtained from my fieldwork in the two religious courts of Tangerang and Serang.

Women's Post-divorce Rights and Men's Enduring Financial Responsibility

The awarding of post-divorce property rights to women stems from the Islamic ruling regarding the husbands' obligation to support their wives when they enter into the marital contract. Wives have the right to property in the form of financial support from their husbands throughout their marital relationship. Beside their share of inheritance upon the death of their husbands, women have at least three rights: to the dowry awarded at the wedding, to financial support throughout the marriage, and to *mut'ah*, should an irrevocable divorce occur (Ridha, 1947).

When a Muslim couple separates, most Islamic family legal codes state that women are not entitled to any post-divorce financial support or property settlement on the grounds that women have already exhausted their share by being sheltered, clothed, and fed by their husbands during their marriage. However, women divorced under *talak* (husband-filed divorce) are entitled to three months of spousal support during the religiously prescribed post-divorce waiting period, known as *iddah* maintenance (Tucker, 2008). Therefore, women's rights to property after divorce include *iddah* maintenance, *mut'ah*, and a share of their husband's estate upon his death. Another form of support that is granted to women is financial support for their children, when the women are awarded custody rights.

The granting of *iddah* maintenance is strongly related to the types of divorce and the court proceedings, and thereby to the judicial decisions. Divorce can be filed by either the husband or the wife, referred to as *talak* (husband-filed divorce) and *khuluk* (wife-filed divorce). When a wife files a divorce, a monetary compensation must be paid to the husband once the divorce is agreed upon (Bowen, 2003). The type of divorce file determines the type of court proceeding and impacts the husband's responsibilities towards his wife.

The *Kompilasi* includes the term '*cerai gugat*' (divorce petition) alongside *khuluk*, which leads me to conclude that not all divorces filed by wives are treated as *khuluk* and therefore monetary compensation to the husband is not always required. Nonetheless this distinction has not been well understood by all judges and results in their biased understanding of how the type of divorce impacts women's post-divorce rights to financial payment. Therefore, while I understand that wives should be awarded rights to *iddah* maintenance when they petition for divorce in a non-*khuluk* manner (where financial compensation to the man is not due), judges tend to dismiss the wife's right to *iddah* maintenance arguing that her filing for divorce results in the loss of that right.

Post-divorce rights and responsibilities of both parties are regulated in Indonesia by the 1974 Marriage Law. In addition, rules for awarding child custody, *iddah* maintenance, and *mut'ah* are specified in the *Kompilasi*, the Muslim legal code. The *Kompilasi* (Art. 149) states that if the marriage is dissolved by *talak*, unless the marriage was unconsummated, the husband is obliged to give a proper *mut'ah* to his ex-wife, in the form of goods or money. The husband is also required to provide financial support during the *iddah* waiting period, as well as a dwelling and clothes unless she was divorced for *bain* (irrevocable divorce) or has been considered disobedient, and as long as she is not pregnant.[1] The husband is also advised to pay *mut'ah* even if the wife files for divorce. To Welchman, this ruling is aimed at deterring husband from arbitrarily exercising unilateral divorce and at compensate the wife for the injury she has sustained (Welchman, 2007).

It seems that post-divorce rights are well administered and that women's legal status has improved. Nonetheless, since these provisions on the whole still follow Islamic traditional law, questions arise as to whether they are sufficient to protect women today. The provision to exclude a so-called disobedient wife from access to post-divorce maintenance (*iddah* maintenance and *mut'ah*) suggests that reforms have been insufficient. Judges in practice tend to refer to different standards in determining a wife's 'disobedience', and in some cases where women left the marital home due to her husband's maltreatment they were considered by the judge to be disobedient, resulting in her loss of post-divorce maintenance.

Indonesian family law may reflect confusion among scholars over the precise meaning of the terms '*iddah*' and 'divorce'. Pereira (2000) has commented on the confusion over the two terms, stating that *iddah* is actually a continuation of marriage, being a waiting period during which the declaration of divorce may be revoked. In her view, during this period the wife and husband continue to be in a legally married state, thus the question of *mut'ah* does not arise, as the wife still has the right to maintenance. In a husband-initiated divorce, once the *iddah* period is over and the divorce becomes effective, post-divorce maintenance is due. In other words, Pereira queries the need for a husband to provide post-divorce maintenance during the *iddah* period, as the marriage is still ongoing. She records that the Muslim family laws of Egypt and Jordan have rightly distinguished between the *iddah* maintenance and *mut'ah*, which she identifies as post-divorce maintenance, not a gift of consolation (Pereira, 2000). In Indonesian family law, as it is meant to be a gift of consolation and is

---

1   Article 149 of the *Kompilasi*. See also Article 152.

paid also within the waiting period, the *mut'ah* amount is small and therefore inadequate to cover the wife's post-divorce financial needs; it is also limited by the husband's capacity to pay.

In addition to the above-mentioned rights, under Islamic legal doctrine, fathers are obliged to financially support their children in all marital circumstances. Dissolution of the marriage by divorce does not free fathers of their responsibilities to provide financial support for their children. In Indonesia, when marriage ends, fathers are obliged to provide financial support for their children according to their financial capacity until the children reach their adulthood and can support themselves or they reach the age of 21.[2] Unlike *iddah* maintenance, financial maintenance for children must always be paid no matter what type of divorce is effective.

The obligation to provide financial support for the children is still binding even when the marriage is dissolved by the death of the husband, and is to be taken over by his family members. This provision is to protect the children's right to property and to assure that they are raised with sufficient financial support. Even in cases in which the mothers work, have financial resources, and may contribute, they are not burdened with the children's financial support.

Iddah Maintenance and *Mut'ah*: Procedural Reform versus Financial Realities

Iddah maintenance and *mut'ah* cases in Islamic courts are not stand-alone cases; they tend to be part of divorce cases. Even when they are filed separately after the divorce proceedings have been completed, they still relate to the decisions made in the divorce case and the nature of the divorce itself.

It was not difficult to find cases of *iddah* and *mut'ah* to observe, as they were almost as frequent as divorce cases filed by husbands. As previously discussed, wives' rights to *iddah* maintenance and *mut'ah* in divorces initiated by their husbands are now quite well protected by law and most of the wives interviewed were aware of their rights. In all of the 18 cases of husband-initiated divorce cases I observed in the Tangerang Religious Court, the judges ruled that the husbands should pay *iddah* maintenance and *mut'ah* to their ex-wives. Many judges assumed that these payments had not yet been (fully or partially) finalized by the husbands. The husbands on the other hand often ignored the

---

2 Article 156 (2) of the *Kompilasi*.

ruling and their obligation to make these payments. As a result, the rulings are not well executed and the wives' rights are not well protected in practice.

Enlightened by notions of justice and the protection of rights acquired over a number of training workshops, judges are now aiming to better implement their rulings and have therefore attempted to make husbands meet their payment obligations. Judges of the Tangerang and Serang religious courts have required husbands to make the payments in court, submitting payment of the *iddah* maintenance and *mut'ah* before the judge. In an even stronger measure, the judges of these two courts, as well as those of the religious courts in Aceh, Padang, and Makassar (Salim et al., 2009), have tended to demand that husbands make the payments before they are permitted to pronounce the divorce formula in court, thereby finalizing the divorce.[3] This attitude of the judges has been very much motivated by the procedural reforms that have been introduced by the Supreme Court through its Circular Letter. As Lindsey elaborated, since 2008 there have been a number of reforms made by the government as to improve access to justice for women and poor people (Lindsey and Sumner, 2010). Prodeo, Posbakum and Circuit Court are among them. The Supreme Court has also warned the judges to realize easier access to justice for women and recommend the judges require husbands to award iddah maintenance within the hearing.

Yet, the judges of the Tangerang and Serang religious courts are also flexible, trying to be realistic and to adapt to the husbands' actual financial state. When they see that a husband has financial problems, judges usually allow him to pronounce the divorce formula without requiring payment at court but they still emphasise the woman's rights and warn the husband to meet his obligations. The judges are concerned that if they are too rigid and strict, only allowing husbands to declare the divorce formula upon the payment made by husband at court, the wives would be disadvantaged as they would be left with an unclear legal status, which might last for several months.

Judges may also make frequent allowances for husbands' finances, disregarding the amounts claimed by wives and deciding on amounts they deem better suited to the husbands' financial capabilities.[4] Therefore, although changes in

---

3   Based on notes on hearings held in the religious courts of Serang and Tangerang and interviews with a number of judges in Serang and Tangerang, in September, October, and November 2010. (Editors' note: Bowen and Salim found the same tendency in 2012 in Aceh and Makassar; making divorce conditional on payment *in most cases* seems to have become accepted practice in at least these jurisdictions.)

4   Based on notes on hearings held in the religious courts of Serang and Tangerang and analysis of a number of judgements issued by these two courts.

judges' attitudes have, to some extent, helped improve justice for women, a number of issues, such as economic and procedural issues, mean that many husbands still do not partially or completely fulfil their legal obligations to their wives (Nurlaelawati, 2013; van Huis, 2011, p. 246). Thus, women feel the need to negotiate with their husbands and the judges to achieve their goals.

Judicial Discretion and Women's Negotiation: Narrative Cases

Two cases will be discussed below to illustrate how husbands understand their legal duties, how wives argue and negotiate at court, and how judges establish and maintain their authority during court hearings.

Judicial Discretion and a Courageous Woman: Sofyan vs Rahmah

I attended nine hearings of husband-filed divorces in the Tangerang and Serang religious courts, two of which illustrate very clearly the above-mentioned judicial discretion.[5] The first case was heard in the Tangerang religious court and demonstrates how judges reach their decision and employ their great authority to decide what they consider to be just for both the wife and husband.[6] The husband, Sofyan [pseudonym], wished to divorce his wife, Rahmah [pseudonym], and the case was examined over several hearings. At the hearing, I attended the husband was permitted to pronounce the divorce formula and was required to pay his wife's post-divorce payments. The hearing opened with the confirmation of a number of agreements made in the previous hearing on the issue of post-divorce rights to be recognized by the husband, including payment of financial maintenance during the *iddah* waiting period and *mut'ah*. There was no need for an agreement on child support, as they had no children. Once the judges understood that the wife and husband had reached agreement on the total payments due, the judges asked the husband if he had the money ready and the husband responded positively. Without being prompted,

---

5 Each case generally is decided over three hearings. The first hearing is to clarify the case details and any possibility for reconciliation, the second hearing is to discuss the evidence, and the third is to reach a judgement. However, due to the detailed issues to be investigated, particularly in the second hearing, the case may take up to eight sessions to resolve. In the case of a husband-petitioned divorce, after the judges issue the decision to approve the petition, they schedule a hearing for the declaration of the divorce formula. For the details of the procedure see Nakamura, 1983; see also Nurlaelawati, 2010, p. 186.

6 This case is also briefly mentioned in my chapter 'Sharia-based laws in Indonesia: The legal position of women and children in Banten and West Java', in van Dijk (2015), which discusses the case as an example of women's improved access to justice.

the husband submitted the money to the clerk who immediately checked the amount submitted, then passed it to Rahmah. She received the money without checking it, as the chief judge had advised. After the money had been paid, the chief judge permitted the husband to pronounce the divorce formula. The hearing was then closed and the litigants shook the judges' hands and were dismissed.[7]

After about one hour Rahmah approached the chief judge. She tried to verify the ruling on *iddah* maintenance and stated that she had just realised that the amount she had received was not as she had proposed. It seemed she had not focussed well on the judges' decision about her financial rights and mentioned that she had asked for more than what she had received that day. Looking most disappointed, she said that she had agreed to divorce provided her husband met her requests. The chief judge responded in a relaxed fashion, saying he remembered the amount she had requested but had found it unrealistically high. He also mentioned that he had mentioned this in the previous session and had understood her to realize this. He also told her that deciding that Sofyan could not afford to pay the amount Rahmah had requested, the judges had lowered the amount due, arguing that it was illogical to demand that he pay a large sum of money that both the husband and wife acknowledged could not be met. Finally, to end the conversation with Rahmah and her father, the chief judge said that the judges could fulfil either the whole petition or part of it and reminded Rahmah of her right to appeal prior to the final hearing where the divorce declaration was pronounced.

Rahmah's father, who had accompanied her in court, said that he was unaware of his daughter's right to appeal the ruling prior to divorce. It may also be true that the father and daughter did not know that they could appeal the case to a higher court. The father admitted that they were not well informed on this matter and had not realized that their demands had not been fully met in the judges' ruling. While the father was still complaining Rahmah began to cry loudly, her face partially hidden by her white headscarf, which attracted the attention of other people in court.

This case shows that the wife was quite aware that she had financial rights and was confident enough to demand them. However, she perhaps lacked experience in court and was not fully aware of the judges' discretion to rule that she be paid less or not at all. It also demonstrates how women are often disadvantaged by their husbands' unilateral decision to divorce. Although wives in husband-filed divorce cases are entitled to receive *iddah* maintenance and

---

7 Based on notes of the 5 October 2010 hearing in the Tangerang religious court.

mut'ah, they may face challenging economic circumstances once they are divorced. From my observations of this case, these were Rahmah's concerns and why she felt so aggrieved by the ruling and this also conveys that although many consider that women in Indonesia enjoy greater status in term of economy (Robinson, 1988), many women remain to bargain with and rely on men.

Judicial Discretion and an Agreeable Woman: Subekti vs Sulastri

The second case concerns a woman, Sulastri [pseudonym], who had been divorced by her husband, Subekti [pseudonym]. Sulastri came to court as a defendant. Her husband was seeking divorce on the grounds that she had not fulfilled her duties as a wife. At the hearing I attended, the husband's divorce petition seemed to have been granted and negotiations were being discussed about the post-divorce payments, based on the agreement reached in the hearing one week earlier.

Sulastri seemed to be strongly aware of her post-divorce rights and demanded that her husband fulfil several financial obligations. She had noted all that was due her after divorce and had also noted certain financial payments that she should have received when she was married but had not. The court recorded her claims, repeating them in the hearing I attended. They included: (1) a compensation payment of Rp. 50,000,000 for her broken heart, (2) financial support of Rp. 2,000,000 for periods when her husband was absent during the marriage, (3) Rp. 1,500,000 for monthly child support for her son, (4) Rp. 2,000,000 for *iddah* maintenance, and (5) Rp. 2,000,000 for the last two months of *arisan*[8] payments that she owed.

The judges evaluated her claims carefully one by one. Upon considering her demand for compensation for her broken heart, the chief judge stated that he understood that it was a normal and rational feeling, but viewed it as hard to quantify in financial terms. The judges found the claim to be excessive, illogical, and not recognized by law. They sought a physiological clarification of the evidence of the existence of such a feeling. It is interesting that judges did not translate this demand as form of *mut'ah*, nor did they propose that Sulastri be paid a minor amount, acceptable to the husband. When she realized that the judges did not recognize her grounds for payment, Sulastri withdrew her claim and it was dismissed.

Before issuing their final ruling, the judges asked Subekti what he thought about the claims, and he stated that he was ready to make the payments his wife

---

8 *Arisan* is a social gathering where all the members save money to form community savings from which each of them in turn gets loans.

WOMEN'S FINANCIAL RIGHTS AFTER DIVORCE IN INDONESIA

demanded, except for the *arisan*, which he would pay but at a lower amount. After some deliberation and evaluation of the case, the judges decided what they considered to be just and issued their judgement. Their decision shows that the judges took into account the husband's financial situation, reducing the payment amount for each demand, except for the *arisan* payment, which was to be paid in full.

The judges explained their decision was based on what the husband could realistically afford with his stated salary of Rp. 1,500,000 per month. They declared the husband could not realistically meet his wife's demands and they agreed to an amount close to what was proposed by the husband. However, they also reminded him that child support was payable for the required period set by law, until the child became financially independent or reached adulthood. They also reminded him that he could extend his *iddah* maintenance for his wife even after the *iddah* period had ended. The wife seemed to accept the judges' decision, without any sign of disappointment. The fact that she kissed her husband after the hearing ended, which she called the last kiss, illustrates her agreement to the judges' ruling. The judges then asked the husband to make his payments in court at the next hearing for the declaration of the divorce formula, to which he responded affirmatively.[9] However, as I did not attend the last hearing, I do not know if he did so.

These two cases essentially indicate a reasonable result for wives with regard to *iddah* maintenance and *mut'ah* payments compared to what they would have received before this procedural reform. However, payments awarded are not always as demanded or expected, and sometimes not in full accordance with the rulings. Some other cases show that more serious problems may remain. From my interviews with a number of husbands and judges, I concluded that many men avoid making their obligated payments due to economic problems and their own ignorance. Many men who fail to make payments at court simply pay no maintenance at all, as they view the relationship over and claim to be too poor. Many wives in fact do not expect the payments to be made, as they know their husbands' character and financial situation. This case shows that women often consider themselves as powerful agent, which, according to Errington (1990), does not only concern economy but also prestige in social life.

Although husbands are aware of their obligations as stated in the court decisions, many still choose not to pay, considering the payments to constitute a religious and not a state obligation, with a sanction not to be faced until the

---

9   Based on notes from the 21 September 2010 Serang religious court hearing.

hereafter. This leads men to ignore their obligation of such payments on the grounds that they are poor,[10] which results in a weak overall implementation of the rulings.

Problems with Implementing Child Support

Financial support for children following divorce is another rights given to women by law. When women are awarded custody of their children, by law the children's father must contribute financially to their upbringing. With regard to the issue of custody, Indonesian state law regulates that, when parents separate, custody of children under 12 is awarded to mothers and children aged over 12 can choose which parent to live with. Although the law is clear in this matter, women may face two issues in custodial cases: first, despite the mother's rights by law, she may still lose custody of her children under age 12, and her children over 12 might choose to live with their father; andsecond, she may struggle for the successful implementation of the courts' decision to award her custody. Although many women face problems of the first kind, more women are awarded custody of their children.[11] By law, child support must be paid by the fathers until the children attain the age of 21. Just as in the case of *iddah* maintenance payments, rulings on child support payments are often not well executed, and in fact may be worse. To achieve better implementation when the mother has been awarded custody, judges have attempted to make the father pay at least one month's child support at the time the *iddah* maintenance payment is made. Generally, judges have made good progress in this regard. In fact, of the 37 collected decisions from the religious courts of Tangerang, Serang, and Cianjur, and six hearings on husband-filed divorce at the religious courts of Serang and Tangerang on cases involving child custody, the fathers in all of the cases were obliged to contribute to the upbringing of children under the mothers' custody. In one of the six divorce case hearings, the father had to provide the first month of child support with the *iddah* maintenance payment before he was permitted to pronounce the divorce in court.

---

10   Interviews with a number of male litigants and judges of the courts of Tangerang and Serang.

11   For detailed discussion of the issue, see Nurlaelawati 2013.

Religious Excuses and Weak Mechanisms

However, although judges have moved to better protect these rights, a number of fathers still do not fulfil their obligations. Besides problems due to financial factors, many men view child support, like *iddah* maintenance, as a religious instead of state matter, and have not paid (Nurlaelawati, 2013, p. 246). The lack of an adequate mechanism for execution has worsened the situation and brought about a wider ignorance concerning the payment of child support.

The following case of Komar, his wife Siti [pseudonyms] and their two children illustrates the problem. Siti had been informed by people who knew her husband that he was cheating on her with another woman. She confronted her husband, who admitted to having an affair with a woman he had known for a year. Komar excused his behaviour by saying that his wife had not treated him well and that she had not respected his wishes in regard to housing. Komar then went to court and filed for divorce. Siti, whose heart was broken, did not try to prevent her husband from divorcing her, although she did not agree that everything her husband said was true. She sought custody of their two children and Rp. 1,500,000 in *iddah* maintenance plus Rp. 600,000 in child support. Her demands for *iddah* maintenance and child support were approved, but the husband petitioned to have custody of one of the children. The judges decided to award custody of one child, aged seven, to the mother and the other, aged 12, to the husband. The wife's monthly child support payments were therefore reduced to Rp. 300,000. Siti accepted all the rulings to ease the divorce process.

When I interviewed Siti she had been divorced for one year and she said that she no longer received regular child support and did not expect to receive more than a small amount from her ex-husband each school term. She tried to accept this by understanding that he had remarried, which affected his financial situation.[12] Her moderate response to her ex-husband's position was also influenced by the fact that he had custody of her other child. This of course is no legal excuse for the father to ignore his duty, as child support should be paid no matter what the financial and marital condition of the father is. However, Siti and Komar both viewed these obligations as religious rather than legal, and thought that they could be delayed – even though Komar agreed that if he did not support his children he would be punished in the hereafter.

Poorly enforced mechanisms for execution represent the main problem with child support. Women lack the authority to insist on the full implementation of the court ruling, which has led Siti, for example, to disregard her rights in this

---

12   Interview with Siti, Tangerang, 14 September 2012.

matter. Unlike *iddah* maintenance, child support rights endure for years and cannot be paid all at once, so enforcement would require a solid, integrated system. Siti has not considered taking this matter to court, as it would involve her spending time, energy, and money. Although the child support requirement was included in the court ruling and therefore constituted a legal claim, the husband interpreted it to be a religious matter, and therefore not binding duty. Siti told me her former husband had excused himself by saying he was already supporting one child, which he considered as sufficient. Furthermore, he said, he also had a new wife to support.

Bilateral Kinship and Extended Families' Financial Support

In my view, Siti's attitude reflects her awareness and understanding, like many other women, of their husbands' general lack of support in child maintenance, although this did not stop her from filing for custody when divorced. The bilateral kinship system that applies in most regions of Indonesia as noted by some researchers (Kuchiba et al, 1979; Fox, 1976; Errington, 1990), means that a woman can always rely on her family of birth to provide financial support, which may have contributed to Siti's attitude. When I discussed the grounds and strategies of women in winning divorce in my previous publication (Nurlaelawati, 2013), I noted that there are two kinds of backgrounds that shape attitudes and conduct in divorce: particular and general grounds. One of the general grounds for divorce is the bilateral kinship system. In the regions where this kinship system applies, women, who mostly acknowledge their husbands' unwillingness to make child support payments after divorce and realize that they may find themselves in a predicament, are safe in the knowledge that they would be able to rely on their extended families. They are therefore not worried about getting divorced and custody of their children. With their families providing support, they believe they can cope with the financial challenges resulting from divorce. In fact, after her divorce Siti returned to her parents and is raising her son with their assistance.

Women Being *Nashiz* and on Filing Divorce: Injustice in the Loss of Rights

Discussing sanctions imposed by Islamic law, Septiani (2012) notes that women can receive sanctions, such as losing their rights to maintenance, if they are deemed disobedient (*nashiz*) as grounds for divorce, that Moors (1995) refers to as 'gender contract'. Women can be deemed disobedient if proved to have disobeyed their husbands, for example, by leaving the marital home. I found in my analysis of court decisions that unfortunately judges did often not attempt to investigate why wives left their marital home but merely judged them disobedient for doing so.[13]

In one of the decisions I reviewed, a husband filed for divorce and alleged his wife had disobeyed him. He told the court that she had left him several times and had ignored his objections to her leaving the home. He added that he had been patient and tolerated her. Interestingly his wife told the court that it was him who often left the marital home. She argued that she had left home because her husband often did not return home. Once confronted, the husband responded that he did not return home as his wife did not treat him well and he got bored staying at home. While it was not very clear, even to judges, who had triggered the marital tensions, the judges concluded that the couple could no longer be united and the marriage could no longer be sustained, to which both parties agreed. Arguing that the wife should not leave the marital home without her husband's permission under any condition, except if her life was endangered, the judges concluded that the wife had committed disobedience or *nusyuz*. It was clear to the judges that the wife had indeed left home, as she had admitted it, but it was difficult to prove that it was the husband's attitude that had led the wife to leave home. Thus, the judges felt that *nushuz* had been committed and therefore the wife had no right to *iddah* maintenance or *mut'ah*.

By law wives also lose their right to maintenance when they initiate divorce. Generally, judges will not make husbands pay maintenance in divorce cases filed by wives and in so doing they refer to *Kompilasi* Article 149.[14] In some cases, however, judges will occasionally consider awarding maintenance to wives if they include such claims in their petition. Judges may also decide that husbands should make maintenance payments but stress that the payment is not based on legal doctrine but is a religious obligation. In one hearing I attended, where a woman named Nur'aini [pseudonym] sued for divorce, the judges demonstrated such considerations. They decided to award Nur'aini the right to *iddah* maintenance, although they understood that it was not required by state law. When they read the decision at the final hearing, they firmly stated that the payment obligation included in the decision was not based based on state law but on '*hukum agama*' (religious law).[15]

---

13   Based on analysis on the decisions issued by the three courts of Tangerang, Serang, and Cianjur. See, for example, decisions No. 99/Pdt.G/2008/PA Tng and No. 410/Pdt.G/2008/PA Srg and 0097/Pdt.G/2008/PA Tng.

14   See for example decision No. 209/Pdt.G/2009/PA-Srg.

15   See decision No. 916/ Pdt.G/2010/PA-Tgr. (Editors' note: the use of "hukum" to refer to both state law, some of which is based on Islam, and the legal dimensions of Islam, allows a

Conclusion

This discussion of women's post-divorce rights demonstrates that financial support is one of the issues that arises after the marriage has dissolved. As I have discussed elsewhere, recently, due to a number of trainings, legal aid services, and legal Courses by both formal legal institutions such as Courts and Offices of Religious Affairs and informal institutions, more Indonesian women know their rights, although their knowledge may be limited. Some women ignore their rights and do not demand they be fulfilled, but many fight for their rights and attempt to persuade the judges when they present their cases in court.

Fortunately, many judges have been sensitized toward gender issues and attempted to protect women's rights. The rise in gender sensitivity amongst judges has been coupled with procedural reform in this field. In fact, judges have required men to bring their money and make their payments at court, which has led women to be more optimistic about the courts' ability to protect their rights. Nevertheless, the fact that many men cannot afford to pay much has meant that full protection of women's rights has not been fully realized.

Indonesia still has serious economic problems, which have contributed to weak implementation of the law and to disappointment for women with regard to their financial support. Currently, judges cannot force men to make payment in court, as there are no regulations requiring this. Judges have argued that a man's failure to meet his financial obligations should not block his right to pronounce the divorce formula. Some judges forced the husband to delay pronouncement of the divorce formula until he made payment, but if husbands cannot pay and the divorce is postponed this does not benefit wives either, as their legal status becomes uncertain.

The perception of some husbands that *iddah* maintenance and *mut'ah* payments are merely religious obligations and thus unenforceable, has also contributed to the weak implementation of the law. Therefore, although legislative reforms have been made by the state to improve justice for women, and judges have attempted to provide women better protection of their rights, women remain wronged. The implementation of financial support for children in custody cases is even worse because fathers' obligation to provide financial support for their children endures for years and requires more money in total. Above all, the relations between the divorced couple may be not amicable. In conclusion, although more women are winning more financial supports,

---

phrase such as "hukum Islam" to be ambiguous, a feature on which these judges were likely relying: the payments are required by the norms and rules of Islam, but not those encoded in Indonesian law.)

it was not without difficulties. Finally, despite a number of attempts to protect women's rights, various factors have prevented women from fully accessing their rights to financial support as defined by law.

Bibliography

Bowen, J. (2003). *Islam, law and equality in Indonesia: An anthropology of public reasoning*. Cambridge, England: Cambridge University Press.

Cammack, M. (1999). Inching toward equality: Recent developments in Indonesian inheritance law. *Indonesian Law and Administration Review, 5(1), 19–50*.

Cammack, M.E., Donovan, H., & Heaton, T.B. (2007). Islamic divorce law and practice in Indonesia. In R.M. Feener & M.E. Cammack (Eds.), *Islamic law in contemporary Indonesia* (pp. 112–114). Cambridge, MA: Harvard University Press.

Errington, Shelly. (1990). "Recasting Sex, Gender and Power: A Theoretical and Regional Overview", in *Power and Difference: Gender in Island Southeast Asia*, ed. by Jane Monnig Atkinson and Shelly Errington. Stanford, CA: Stanford University Press.

Fox, Robin. (1976) *Kinship and Marriage: An Anthropological Perspective*. Harmondsworth: Penguin.

Hirsch, S.F. (1998). *Pronouncing and preserving: Gender and the discourses of disputing in African Islamic court*. Chicago, IL: The University of Chicago.

Mir-Hosseini, Z. (2006). Muslim women's quest for equality: Between Islamic law and feminism. *Critical inquiry, 32(4), 629–645*.

Mir-Hosseini, Z. (2013). Justice, equality and Muslim family laws: New ideas, new prospects. *Gender and equality in Muslim family law: Justice and ethics in the Islamic Legal Process, 7–36*. New York, NY: I.B. Tauris & Co. Ltd.

Kuchiba, M., Tsubouchi, Y., & Maede, N. (1979). *Three Malay villages: Sociology of paddy growers in West Malaysia*. Honolulu, HI: Hawaii University Press.

Nakamura, H. (1983). *Divorce in Java*. Yogyakarta, Indonesia: Gadjah Mada University Press.

Nasution, K. (2002). *Status wanita di Asia Tenggara: Studi terhadap perundang-undangan perkawinan Muslim kontemporer di Indonesia dan Malaysia*. Jakarta, Indonesia: INIS.

Nurlaelawati, E. (2010). *Modernization, tradition and identity: The Kompilasi Hukum Islam and legal practice in the Indonesian religious courts*. Amsterdam, Netherlands: Amsterdam University Press.

Nurlaelawati, E. (2013). Indonesian Muslim women at court: Reform, strategies and pronouncement of divorce. *Islamic Law and Society, 20* (3), 242–271.

Pereira, F. (2000). Post-divorce maintenance for Muslim women and the Islamist discourse. *WLUML Dossier 22 November 1999, 1–4*.

Ridhā, R. (1947). *Tafsīr al-Manār* (vol. 2). Beirut, Lebanon: Dar ul-Fikr.

Robinson. Kathryn, (1988), "What Kind of Freedom is Cutting Your Hair? Class and Gender in a Peripheral Capitalist Economy", in *Development and Displacement: Women in Southeast Asia*, ed. by Glen Chandler, Norma Sullivan, and Jan Branson. Clayton, Vic.: Centre of Southeast Asian Studies, Monash University.

Salim, A., Nurlaelawati, E., Marcoes, L., & Sayuti, W. (2009). *Demi keadilan dan kesetaraan: Dokumentasi program sensitivitas gender Hakim Agama.* Jakarta, Indonesia: PUSKUMHAM.

Septiani, R. (2012). *Sanksi terhadap istri dalam hukum formal keluarga Islam: Perspektif keadilan gender di Indonesia.* Jakarta, Indonesia: Pustaka Anak Negeri.

Soewondo, N. (1977). The Indonesian marriage law and its implementing regulation. *Archipel, 13* (1), 283–294.

Sumner, C., & Lindsey, T. (2011). Courting reform: Indonesia's Islamic courts and justice for the poor. *International Journal for Court Administration, 4(1), 3–16.*

Tucker, J. (2008). *Women, family and gender in Islamic law.* Cambridge, England: Cambridge University Press.

van Dijk, K. (2015). *Islam, politics, and change: The case of Indonesia.* Leiden, Netherlands: Leiden University Press.

van Huis, S. (2011). Akses terhadap hak-hak pascaperceraian bagi perempuan bercerai di Cianjur. In W. Berenschot (Ed.), *Akses terhadap keadilan: Perjuangan masyarakat miskin dan kurang beruntung untuk menuntut hak di Indonesia* (pp. 233–253). Jakarta, Indonesia: HuMA.

Welchman, Lynn. (2007). *Women and Muslim Family Law in Arab States: A Comparative Overview of Textual Development and Advocacy.* Amsterdam: Amsterdam University Press.

Laws and Regulations

Law No. 1 of 1974 on Marriage
Presidential Instructions No. 1 of 1991 on Compilation of Islamic Law

Court Decisions

Serang Religious Court Decision No. 410/Pdt.G/2008/PA-Srg
Serang Religious Court Decision No. 209/Pdt.G/2009/PA-Srg
Tangerang Religious Court Decision No. 99/Pdt.G/2008/PA-TNG
Tangerang Religious Court Decision No. 97/Pdt.G/2008/PA-TNG
Tangerang Religious Court Decision No. 916/Pdt.G/2010/PA-TGR

CHAPTER 6

Mut'ah and *Iddah*

Post-divorce Payment Practices in Aceh

Abidin Nurdin

Matters dealing with post-divorce payments are not just confined to the practices of the Indonesian Islamic Courts but are a feature of the Islamic world in general. In Morocco, a husband who unilaterally divorces his wife is obliged to pay her *mut'ah*, sometimes called a consolation gift. The size of the payment depends on the husband's financial circumstances and the wife's social status (Muzdhar & Nasution, 2003, p. 113). South Yemen laws prescribe a compensation payment similar to *mut'ah*, to be paid by the party found responsible for the divorce. If the husband is declared guilty he must pay (no more than) one year's living expenses; if the wife is declared guilty, the amount due must not exceed the value of her dowry. A similar provision can be found in Turkey (Muzdhar & Nasution, 2003, p. 78). In Brunei as well, should a husband divorce his wife, she may request the court to be granted a payment calculated as fit and proper according to Islamic law, after the judge has heard the testimony of both parties (Supriyadi & Mustafa, 2009, p. 153).

In Singapore, the religious court has the right to determine the *nafkah mut'ah* amount, called 'maintenance', which the husband must pay to the wife during the *iddah* period,[1] and the *nafkah mut'ah* amount, which is intended to help heal the hurt of the divorced party. Usually the amount is relatively standard and is determined through the agreement of both parties. Since 1984 the obligatory *mut'ah* payment has been set at around 1 USD per day from the wedding day to the date of divorce. This means, for example, if a couple has been married for ten years, and the husband divorces his wife without clear grounds, the wife is entitled to claim an amount of Singapore $ 2,650 as *mut'ah* (Hasyim, 1993, p. 116).

In Indonesia, there have been numerous studies concerning this issue by researchers and scholars. They may be divided into three categories: firstly, fiqh-based studies (Islamic jurisprudence) norms, without examining what occurs

---

1 The legally prescribed period during which a woman may not remarry after having been widowed or divorced.

in practice in court. Syarifuddin (2006, p. 322) as well as Nuruddin and Tarigan (2004, p. 249) write that amongst the rights of a wife upon *talak raj'i* (revocable divorce) is the financial support during the *iddah* period when she does not remarry. The amount of supports is similar to the one she received before the divorce, in the form of food, clothing, and accommodation expenses. Further, Ghazaly (2006) explains that a wife who has been obedient and good to her husband during the *iddah* period following a *talak raj'i* divorce is entitled to receive accommodation, food, and spending money from her former husband. However, a disobedient and ungrateful wife is not entitled to receive anything (p. 266).

The second category is judicial studies, or studies of payments that employ *ushul fiqh* (Islamic legal theory) and the jurisprudence from the decisions of religious courts in Indonesia. Effendi M. Zein (2004) studies various Islamic family law matters, including divorce suits arising from a husband's lack of support for his family, as well as claims for payment of maintenance and/or lump sums. Zein writes that there are two possible reasons why a husband may not pay the required post-divorce payments: he may be unable financially, or he may be unwilling. In the first case the husband cannot be forced to pay until his personal financial situation recovers, while in the second case the judge may seize husband's property and award it to the wife.

The third category is anthropological-ethnographic studies, namely studies of post-divorce payments that focus on court institutional practices analyzed anthropologically. Duriati (2009) says that the practice of making payments to the wife in the Semarang religious court depends on whether the wife who files a suit or is happy to forego her rights (p. 65). If the wife files a suit then the judges must ensure the husband fulfils his legal duties, but if she does not sue then her husband is legally absolved of any responsibilities. Meanwhile, according to Sarizal (2012) in the Banda Aceh religious court the judges consider the husband's financial means when they determine the *mut'ah* and *iddah* payments due. Ihsan (2006) outlined the *mut'ah* payment practice for a husband employed as a civil servant who divorced in the Takengon religious court (pp. 51–66). He concluded that the judges considered the following factors in determining the amount of *mut'ah* to be paid after their divorce: (1) the husband's duty to make a *mut'ah* payment to his wife, and (2) the existence of statutory stipulations allowing for the provision of *mut'ah* to the wife.

A further, more complete, anthropological study was conducted by Bowen (2003) who concluded that the religious court judgements were better appreciated in Gayo (Central Aceh). These judgements played a role in the heightened respect for and protection of woman's material rights. To understand judicial practice in such matters in Aceh, one can read Salim and colleagues

(2009) who explain that there is a new school of thought amongst judges that stresses the importance of the *sunnah muakkadah* (the strongly recommended words and acts of Muhammad) in interpreting *mut'ah* and *iddah* payment practices, as stated in the 1991 Presidential Instruction No. 1 in the *Kompilasi Hukum Islam* (*Compilation of Islamic Laws*, KHI), where their legal status has been strengthened from *ghairu muakkadah* (not strongly recommended) to *muakkadah* (strongly recommended) (p. 65).

There have indeed been many studies of the *mut'ah* and *iddah* payments, but most have focused on normative and/or juridical aspects, except for those by Duriati, Syahrizal, Ihsan, Bowen, and Salim. These five studies focus on the practice of *mut'ah* and *iddah* payments, as described below. This chapter endeavours to ethnographically analyze, through a legal anthropological approach, the practice of *mut'ah* and *iddah* payments, as they occur in the religious or *shari'a* courts of Banda Aceh and Aceh Besar. It is significant because it is based not just on written court judgements but also field observations in the courtroom, including the arguments and reasoning of the presiding judges in divorce payment cases. The central argument of this chapter is that the judges weigh three factors in determining the amount of *mut'ah* and *iddah* payments: the conduct of the husband and the wife, the wife's need for maintenance, and the husband's ability to pay. For space reasons, I limit my analysis to two of the cases observed.

Women and Property in Aceh

In general, Acehnese women are relatively well positioned to own property under Islamic law and local Acehnese culture and customary law. The Acehnese for example, have the concept of *hareuta peunulang*, which refers to a gift to a daughter from her parents, usually a house, land, or other form of property. *Hareuta peunulang* is a form of protection of women's financial resources for their daughter before she builds a new household with her husband. This is why women in Aceh are also referred to as *'peurumoh'*, meaning house owners. So, should a divorce occur, it is not the woman who must leave the house, but rather the husband, because the house is part of the property that the woman has brought into the marriage. Thus, in this way Acehnese women occupy a position not dissimilar to men.[2] With regard to the ethnographic results from

---

2 Interview with Rusjdi Ali Muhammad, Professor of Islamic Law, the State Islamic Religious Institute, IAIN Ar-Raniry, in Banda Aceh, 30 June 2011.

his study of Pidie society, Abdurrahman (2000) stresses that the purpose of *hareuta peunulang* is to strengthen the Acehnese socio-religious community in general by providing for daughters on the eve of their marriage, and ensuring they are provided for should they unfortunately be deserted by their husbands (p. 42).

In addition to *hareuta peunulang*, Aceh also has the concept of *hareuta seuharkat* or *hareuta syarikat*, meaning joint property: in Javanese, this is called '*gono gini*', in Makassar Buginese '*cakara*'', and in Minangkabau '*harta suarang*'. Division of this joint property can vary but in general it is divided in two: half for the husband and half for the wife (Syahrizal, 2004, p. 275). Variations in the division of joint property are caused by local customs and norms. Acehnese society is largely comprised of farmers who work rice paddies. In Pidie, for example, the division of property is 1:1, equal between the man and woman, while in North Aceh and Aceh Besar, the division is 2:1, with the man receiving two parts and the woman one. This is because, while in Pidie the man and woman do an equivalent work in the paddies, in North Aceh and Aceh Besar their work differs so the portions also differ.[3]

After the 2004 tsunami many cases related to women and property were filed, and several non-governmental organizations emerged to advocate for unrepresented clients, for instance the Bungoeng Jeumpa Foundation (Yayasan Bungoeng Jeumpa or YBJ), which from 2005–2007 covered property issues involving both men and women. These property cases involved issues of: (1) inheritance, (2) land, (3) gifts, (4) joint property, and (5) custody of children. During the 2008–2009 period these cases were solved either by litigation or community deliberations. YBJ provided support and advocacy in seven cases, prior to appearances in court, and support and advocacy in six cases resolved through community deliberations at the *gampong* (kampong) level.[4]

It is interesting to note here the report initiated by the International Development Law Organization (IDLO) in 2006 regarding the practice of formal and informal resolutions of land, inheritance, and custody issues after the tsunami in Banda Aceh and Aceh Besar. The report outlined how, compared to *adat* or customary law functionaries, the *shari'a* court paid better attention to the position of women, particularly in resolving matters of inheritance, land, and custody issues. The *shari'a* court in a practical way provided fresh direction, by, for example, allocating the entire estate of two deceased

---

3 Interview with Muslim Ibrahim, Professor at IAIN Ar-Raniry and Chairman of the Ulama Deliberation Board of the Aceh Province, in Banda Aceh, 19 July 2012.

4 Interview with Wanti Maulidar, Director of Bungong Jeumpa Foundation, in Banda Aceh, 29 June 2011.

MUT'AH AND IDDAH   111

parents to the sole child, a daughter, despite there still being a living uncle, and similarly innovative rulings in child custody cases (Salim, 2006).

Mut'ah and Iddah in Religion and Law

As noted at the outset of this chapter, *mut'ah* is the gift a husband provides to his wife when he divorces her (Mujieb, 1994, p. 233). The gift may consist of clothes, money, jewellery, domestic help, or something else. The size of the gift varies according to the husband's economic situation. *Mut'ah* is the right of every woman who is divorced by her husband, according to the Qur'anic verse, 'And for divorced women is a provision according to what is acceptable – a duty upon the righteous' (al-Baqarah: 241).

The *iddah* payment is an allowance given by a man to his former wife as determined by the court. This payment is to cover the *iddah* waiting period before a woman may legally remarry after divorce or the death of her husband, typically three to four months. This *iddah* period applies to both divorcees and widows and it is intended to allow time to know if the woman is pregnant, and for the husband to consider whether to proceed with the divorce or to take his wife back (Dahlan, 1996, p. 637).

Within an Islamic jurisprudence context, scholars argue that a husband may rightfully take back as his wife the woman he has divorced by *talak raj'i*, meaning after one or two *talak*,[5] without requiring a marriage ceremony (Al-Gharayani, 2007, p. 199). Bearing this in mind, the wife has the right to be provided accommodation by her husband during the *iddah* period, as stated in the Qur'an: 'O Prophet, when ye do divorce women, divorce them at their prescribed periods [iddah]. And count their prescribed periods and fear Allah your Lord. And turn them not out of their houses, nor shall they themselves [be permitted to] leave. Except lest they be guilty of some open lewdness' (al-Thalaq: 1).

Furthermore, according to state law, *mut'ah* and *iddah* are regulated by the 1974 Law No. 1 on Marriage, where it is stated that the court may require the husband to provide living expenses and/or other payments to his former wife (Article 41). The 1991 KHI states the husband must provide his wife: (a) an appropriate *mut'ah*, in the form of money or goods, unless she has been determined *qabla al-dhukhul* (to have had sexual relations); and (b) *nafkah* (main-

---

5   *Talaq* is an Arabic word meaning 'to release' or 'to divorce'. Under Islamic law, *talaq* means 'to untie the matrimonial knot by articulating the word denoting divorce'.

tenance), *maskan* (accommodation), and *kiswah* (clothing) during the *iddah* period, unless she was given a *talak ba'in* (irrevocable divorce) or a *nusyuz* divorce (where she was determined to have disobeyed the lawful wishes or commands of her husband) and is not pregnant (Article 149). The husband must pay *mut'ah* provided that: (a) a *ba'da dukhul* dowry price was not set upon the wife, and (b) the divorce was at the request of the husband (Article 159). *Mut'ah* is commonly provided by the husband unconditionally as stated in Article 158, with the amount adjusted to what is appropriate to the husband's means (Articles 159 and 160).

Similar religious practices related to maintenance payments are also found amongst the Protestant religious community in Indonesia. Simanungkalit (2008) concludes that Protestants follow the applicable state law, the 1974 Law No. 1 on Marriage, or the decision of a district court, whereas the Catholic Church does not acknowledge divorce and thus does not discuss the payment of alimony (p. 67).[6] During the Dutch colonial regime similar legislation existed: Ordinance No. 74 of 1933 on the Marriages of Christians in Java, Minahasa, and Ambon.[7] Article 59, paragraph (2) of this ordinance stated that Christian wives may claim maintenance payments in hearings at the state district court, and if the court supports the wife's claim, the husband must make these payments to her in court.

In essence, post-divorce *mut'ah* and *iddah* payments operate as a form of income insurance for women as well as a guarantee of gender equity in court (Salim, 2009, pp. 66–67). In most divorces, the party more aggrieved is the wife, thus, under Islamic law the husband must pay her an allowance during the mandatory waiting period. Her former husband may, the very next day, marry another woman – a divorcee, widow, or virgin – but a divorced woman tends not to remarry, particularly if she has many children, preferring to focus on the raising and education of her children. For these reasons *shari'a* law offers respite in the form of *mut'ah*.[8]

---

6 Divorce is absolutely forbidden in Catholicism, according to the teachings of Paul in Romans 7:2 in the Bible: 'A wife is bound by law to her husband as long as her husband is alive. However, if her husband dies, she is free from the law that binds her to husband. So as long as her husband is alive she is considered to be adulterous if she becomes the wife of another man; but if her husband is dead, she is free by law, and she is not committing adultery if she becomes another man's wife'.

7 Ordinance of Marriages of Indonesian Christians in Java, Minahasa, and Ambon (Huwelijk-sordonnantie Christen-Indonesier Java, Minahasa, en Amboina, Ord. 15 February 1993) S. 1993 No. 74.

8 Interview with Judge Hurriyah Abubakar of the Banda Aceh *shari'a* court, 23 July 2012.

MUT'AH AND IDDAH

Judges view *mut'ah* and *iddah* payments as a form of protection of women's rights. However, despite being regulated by Government Regulation No. 10/1983, which states that wives of civil servants will receive this kind of financial protection, often payments are not made (Ihsan, 2006, p. 85). If payments are not made, this strongly affects the woman's economic and social situation. If she has children, she may be unable to guarantee them adequate and appropriate levels of education, nutrition, physical health, and financial stability.

Post-divorce Payments in Jantho and Banda Aceh Shari'a Courts

This section discusses two cases of couples from differing economic and educational backgrounds, one from Jantho *shari'a* court and the other from the Banda Aceh *shari'a* court, both courts of first instance within Indonesia's system of Islamic courts.

Jantho Shari'a Court

The case in the Jantho *shari'a* court concerned a husband (36 years old) as the plaintiff and his wife (33 years old) as the defendant. The plaintiff was a civil servant (lecturer) in a university in Aceh with a master's degree, while the defendant was a contract teacher in Lhokseumawe High School who also held a master's degree. The husband's grounds for divorce were that his wife had lived apart from him for over three years as she had chosen to live and work in Lhokseumawe as a high school teacher. The wife's demands, the husband's response, and the judge's decision are summarised in Table 6.1 below.

Glancing at the wife's demands, the husband's response, and the judge's decision, it may be concluded that the judge had determined a relatively small total amount to be paid by the husband. The reasons for this were based on the wife's behaviour, as she had apparently left their home for more than three years, and this fact was admitted by the defendant and corroborated by a number of witnesses. Although the defendant presented several reasons as to why their relationship was inharmonious (*syiqaq*), which she said had compelled her to leave home, the plaintiff had also made various efforts to reunite.[9]

---

9   See decision number 39/Pdt.G/2012/MS-JTH.

114   NURDIN

TABLE 6.1   Divorce case of civil servants in Jantho Shari'a Court

Party	Employment/ wages	Wife's demands	Husband's response	Judge's decision
Husband	Civil servant, wages Rp. 2,590,400/mo.	*Iddah* Rp. 5,000,000	*Iddah* Rp. 2,500,000	*Iddah* Rp. 2,500,000
		Mut'ah Rp. 5,000,000	*Mut'ah* 1 mayam gold (approx Rp. 1,600,000)	*Mut'ah* 1 mayam gold (approx Rp. 1,600,000)
Wife	Contract teacher wages unknown	*Kiswah* Rp. 5,000,000	No *kiswah*	No *kiswah*
		Child support Rp. 2,000,000/mo.	Child support Rp. 700,000/mo.	Child support Rp. 700,000/mo.
Amount		Rp. 17,000,000	Rp. 4,800,000	Rp. 4,850,000

This may be concluded from the facts revealed in the proceedings, exemplified in this exchange between the judge and the plaintiff:

> Judge: Why do you, the plaintiff, wish to divorce your wife? What do you mean you are no longer able to maintain a household together? What was the cause of the disharmony and the quarrels? Were there any reconciliation attempts made with your wife?
>
> Plaintiff: I cannot live like this anymore. Our relationship is no longer harmonious. During our married life from 2007 until now [2012] we often quarrelled, even though sometimes we made up. I actually don't understand for certain but it is clear that we don't understand and accept each other. However, I always tried to find a peaceful way and discuss the issues but quarrels always happened. This is what I cannot bear and what disappoints me. The peak of the quarrels was from June 17, 2008, until now, around three years and six months. The defendant left me; she went to Lhokseumawe and prefers to live there rather than with me. I also tried to make peace and re-unite with my wife. I sent her an SMS several times [4–5 times] to invite her to live together again, but it was not successful. I even contacted our teacher, a professor in Banda Aceh, to help bring

peace between is, also a friend of ours who is a counsellor, and lastly the Office of Religious Issues. These three efforts failed and my wife never wanted to meet up to discuss our lives.

The proceedings reveal that the plaintiff had already attempted to reconcile and live once more with the defendant, but his efforts were refused. This was also strengthened by the testimony of the counsellor, who appeared as a witness for the plaintiff. The counsellor once had tried to contact the defendant by mobile phone but she would not answer, and also tried to persuade her to make peace but she refused.

Then, the judge asked the defendant: 'Is it true that you and the plaintiff are living apart? Since when? And why did you separate from your husband? Were there any efforts to make peace, and what did you do?' The defendant answered:

Yes, your Honour, since June 2008 we were no longer well suited. From the time we sat on our wedding thrones, I already felt that incompatibility. Actually, before marrying, I was already working as a teacher in a high school in Lhokseumawe. When I left my home, I was escorted by the plaintiff to the house of my foster parents in Bireuen. Actually, I also tried to make peace. This is why I reject the statement that I had been contacted for reconciliation by a teacher, friend, and the Religious Office. I was never contacted by them.

In her statement, the defendant admitted that she had left the plaintiff for more than three years and six months, although she offered the excuse that her husband had escorted her when she left the house. However, when she was asked whether there had been any reconciliation attempts, she claimed there had not denied this, although the plaintiff stated he had made efforts and this was supported by witnesses.

The judges found the defendant's admission that she had left home for more than three years as evidence in support of the plaintiff's grounds for divorce, as written in the judgment:

Considering that in the facts found in the proceedings concerning whether or not there were quarrels and disagreements between the plaintiff and the defendant, it was admitted by the defendant herself in her answer, although for reasons different to the grounds presented by the plaintiff, and also strengthened by the plaintiff's witnesses, who testified that it was true that there had been a conflict between the plaintiff and the defendant, resulting in them living apart. The witnesses from the defendant's side also stated that the relationship between the plaintiff and the defendant was not harmonious and that they had separated houses since around 3 years ago, as well as witnesses and the families of the two sides had tried to offer counsel and reconcile them but they failed. Therefore, the panel of judges judged that such a separation of domiciles between husband and wife was an indication of the conflict and quarrels between the plaintiff and the defendant and hence the plaintiff's grounds were proven.[10]

According to the KHI, if a wife leaves her husband for more than two years, that will automatically sever the marriage bond (Article 116, Part B). The wife's behaviour could thus be considered an act of *nusyuz*, which would mean she would not be entitled to receive *nafkah iddah*, *mut'ah*, or *kiswah*. However, the judges did not mention *nusyuz* at all in the decision. This is evidence of their bias towards the woman; by not mentioning *nusyuz*, the implication was that the judges believed the woman would suffer economically and even psychologically as a result of the divorce, and they wanted to avoid this from happening.

According to the plaintiff, the judges' decision that he should pay Rp. 4,850,000 was proper and fulfilled a sense of justice. The plaintiff reasoned that his wife's behaviour led the judges to reduce the payment due from the plaintiff, as her actions demonstrated that she bore responsibility for the failure of the marriage.[11]

The husband's capacity to pay was also part of the judges' consideration. The panel of judges deemed that, according to the principle of propriety and the needs of the defendant, the amount the defendant demanded was too high, and not in keeping with the income level of a civil servant with a monthly wage of Rp. 2,590,400. Therefore, guided by a sense of justice as well as the financial means of the plaintiff, the panel of judges rejected the amount of the defendant's claim.[12] The plaintiff accepted the facts presented in the proceedings, the decision, and the amount he had to pay, and was of the opinion that it was in line with his capacity to pay.[13]

---

10   See decision number 39/Pdt.G/2012/MS-JTH.
11   Interview with plaintiff in divorce case in the Jantho *shari'a* court, Aceh Besar, 26 January 2013.
12   See decision number 39/Pdt.G/2012/MS-JTH.
13   Interview with plaintiff in a divorce case in the Jantho *shari'a* court, Aceh Besar, 26 January 2013.

MUT'AH AND IDDAH

Banda Aceh Shari'a Court

The case in Banda Aceh *shari'a* court concerned a plaintiff (33 years old) and his wife (27 years old), the defendant.[14] The university-educated plaintiff was employed as a non-tenured worker and the defendant was a high school-educated housewife. The husband's grounds for divorce were that there were constant quarrels between them and that the defendant disapproved of his closeness to his parents and siblings. The wife's demands, the husband's response, and the judges' decision are summarised in Table 6.2 below.

The judgment states that the wife's behaviour was in no way improper. She had sacrificed part of her property to help meet the family's economic needs, and she helped support the family by baking cakes and selling them. The real issue was that there was the presence of the third party, namely the parent (mother) of the plaintiff, who had never blessed the relationship between her son and the defendant.

This can be seen in the response included in the judgment, in which the plaintiff declared: 'In the beginning the family life of the plaintiff and defendant was happy and peaceful but from the second month of marriage there were continuous differences and quarrelling and there was no further hope of living peacefully together as a family because, amongst other reasons: (a) the defendant did not wish to be close to the parents and the siblings of the plaintiff; and (b) the family life of the plaintiff and the defendant was no longer harmonious'.[15]

This was then refuted in the defendant's rejoinder:

> It was not true that the defendant disapproved of the plaintiff being close to his parents and siblings. That is an excuse that has no basis in Islamic law, something that has been merely fabricated to meet the required elements of the plaintiff's divorce suit, but rather the truth was that the defendant had allowed the plaintiff to go home to visit his mother and his relatives, as that behaviour is encouraged in Islamic law which we must uphold, and the plaintiff and the defendant came to know each other out of love, not from an arranged marriage. But the plaintiff's mother always forbade the journey of our loving relationship. Before we were married the plaintiff's mother once sought out the defendant seeking to pay her to leave the plaintiff but the defendant refused. Whereas the defendant also helped to earn a living to meet the household needs, baking cakes

---

14   Decision number 267/Pdt.G/2011/MS-Bna.
15   Decision number 267/Pdt.G/2011/MS-Bna.

118 NURDIN

TABLE 6.2 Divorce case of a non-tenured worker

Party	Employment/ wages	Wife's demands	Husband's response	Judges' decision
Husband	Non-tenured worker, no fixed monthly wages	*Iddah* Rp. 15,000,000, *Mut'ah* Rp. 15.000.000, *Kiswah* Rp. 25.000.000	Can only afford to pay Rp. 1,500,000 each of *iddah*, *mut'ah* and *kiswah*, as lacking a regular wage.	*Iddah* Rp. 1,700,000, *mut'ah* Rp. 1,000,000, and No *kiswah*
		Due maintenance Rp. 10,000,000	Due maintenance Rp. 400,000	No maintenance
Wife	Housewife, no information on wages	Dowry owed 4 *mayam* of gold = Rp. 6,000,000	Not recognized	Owes 3 *mayam* = Rp. 4,500,000
		Owed a ring of 1 *mayam* = Rp. 1,000,000	Not recognized	No ring
		Credit in an account in the Bank Syariah Mandiri = Rp. 4,320,000	Not recognized	Changed to credit with PT CCM, based on court evidence. Rp. 1,458,000
Amount		Rp. 76,320,000	Rp. 1,900,000	Rp. 8,658,000

and waking at 4 a.m. to bake them and her parents also provided assistance nearly every month. But within about 10 days after his return from his parents' home the defendant felt changes in him. Has the problem merely been fabricated to fulfil the elements permitting divorce/*talak*?[16]

---

16   Decision number 267/Pdt.G/2011/MS-Bna.

The panel of judges stated that they had listened to the plaintiff's response and the defendant's rejoinder, who, in principle, maintained their respective positions, namely that the plaintiff wanted to divorce the defendant whereas the defendant did not desire divorce, but should the divorce proceed, the defendant demanded the plaintiff pay *iddah*, *mut'ah*, and *kiswah* payments as well as the plaintiff's debts owed to the defendant, as recorded in the defendant's response.

The plaintiff had claimed that he could only afford to pay Rp. 1,900,000 of what the defendant requested. However, as the judges considered the wife's behaviour to be proper, and the husband had secure employment at the Office of Public Works, they determined a relatively high amount, totalling Rp. 8,658,000, to be paid by the plaintiff.[17]

Analysis of the Judges' Decisions

In these two cases, as well as others studied as part of the broader research project, it is apparent that the judges focused on both the moral conduct of the two parties and the husband's financial means. The wife's conduct could be the grounds for divorce if, for example, the wife had betrayed the husband. If such betrayal occurs, the *mut'ah* may not be given to the wife. Of course, the wife's situation is also considered: should it worsen or be impacted badly if payment is not provided, then payments should be given. For example, should a wife be plunged into immoral work such as prostitution for her survival after her divorce, then the judges agree that husband should pay *mut'ah*.[18]

The judges' evaluation of the husband's capacity to pay has a legal impact. A husband, for example, may be ordered to pay the *mut'ah*, *iddah*, and other payments amounting to ten million, when he can only afford to pay five million. If *nafkah* is not paid, and six months elapses, then the case is automatically annulled or invalidated, because six months has passed without the husband pronouncing divorce. Judges do not want their decision to be invalidated because this would leave the wife unsupported; they would prefer to make the husband pay five million to provide legal certainty for the woman, and avoid their decision being voided.[19]

---

17   Decision number 267/Pdt.G/2011/MS-Bna.

18   Interview with Hurriyah Abubakar, judge at the Banda Aceh Shari'a Court, 23 July 2012.

19   Interview with Hurriyah Abubakar, judge at the Banda Aceh Shari'a Court, 23 July 2012; interview with Marlianita, plaintiff's lawyer for a divorce, in Banda Aceh, 5 September 2012.

Government Regulations versus Islamic Law

Divorce by a husband who works as a civil servant is regulated in Government Regulation (PP) No. 10/1983 on Permission for Marriage and Divorce for Civil Servants. Article 8 of that law states: (1) if divorce occurs at the wish of the male civil servant he is obliged to surrender a portion of his wage for the livelihood of this wife and children; (2) the portion of the wages referred to in paragraph (1) is one-third for the male civil servant in question, one-third for his ex-wife, and one-third for their children; (3) if there is no issue from that marriage, the portion of the wages to be surrendered to the former wife is a half of his wage. This regulation was updated by PP No. 45/1990 whose Article 4 states that division of wages to the wife is not granted if the grounds for divorce are due to the wife's adultery and/or cruelty or grievous harm, either physical or psychological; and/or the wife has become an incurable alcoholic, drug addict, or gambler; and/or the wife has deserted the husband for two years running without the husband's permission and without valid cause or due to something beyond her control.

Regarding this regulation, although there was a debate amongst judges and within the courts over what power the courts had to regulate this issue, it is the husband's place of work that withholds any wages, as clarified in the PP. Given the division of authority, the court does not regulate these matters in its decisions, to avoid interfering in matters outside its control. The ex-wife can report to her husband's office, although sometimes this is not implemented in practice; it is dependent on the husband's superior and the accounts department at his office.[20] Judge Surya in the Jantho *shari'a* court argued there were two alternatives; first, an administrative approach, where the matter is surrendered to the husband's office, and second, a legal approach, where the matter must be stated in the court's decision as it originates in the law and must be included in the court's decision.[21]

However, the chief judge at the Aceh provincial *shari'a* court, Hamid Pulungan, considered the government regulation to contravene Islamic law, because the regulation does not specifiy how long the civil servant must pay a portion of his wage. Under Islamic law the *iddah nafkah* must be paid to the wife for three months and 10 days, or the waiting period before the wife remarries. The length of the *iddah* period is not mentioned in the government regulation, just

---

20   Interview with Samsir, high judge in the Aceh provincial *shari'a* court, in Banda Aceh, 16 July 2012.

21   Interview with Surya, vice chair of the Jantho *shari'a* court, Aceh Besar, in Jantho, 25 April 2012.

stating that it is lasts until she remarries. If wife does not remarry for ten years, should the husband still be obliged to pay *nafkah* to his ex-wife? This would contradict Islamic law. Hence judges rarely refer to this government regulation and are loath to consider using it.[22] Thus the Supreme Court unofficially recommended increasing the amount of the *mut'ah* because it is not sustainable for one-third of a husband's wages to be garnished for more than three months.

Judge Surya of the Jantho *shari'a* court held a different view, that the regulation did not contravene fiqh because when a husband married it meant that he was happy to share his wages with his wife. So, it was more a matter of rights, because these rights are not automatically extinguished by the divorce. Moreover, the husband's wages are the joint property of the husband and wife. Thus, the wife's rights to the wages are not summarily annulled. This type of opinion can be categorized as contemporary fiqh.[23]

Judge Surya emphasized further that the one-third wages as *mut'ah nafkah* compensation cannot be in the form of a three-month or lump sum *iddah*. *Mut'ah* is of a general nature (*lex generalis*), while the provision to pay one-third wages is *lex spesialis*, as it refers specifically to civil servants. Thus, this would cause uncertainty, and law requires certainty.[24] The point of uncertainty is that giving one-third of wages to one's ex-wife is a PP (Government Regulation) command but on the other hand it is against Islamic law.

Judge Surya's view that the government regulation was not contrary to fiqh is somewhat courageous, as many judges understand it to be contrary to Islamic law. According to fiqh principles, the husband's obligations only last for the *iddah* period, meaning no more than three months, after which the obligation of the husband no longer exists except for a child. However, according to the PP (government regulation), the ex-husband is obliged to give one-third of his salary until his ex-wife marries someone else. The legal reality is that the government regulation is not employed and its logic considered invalid. Furthermore, the opinion that the *mut'ah* cannot be paid from one-third of the husband's wages was also countered in case number 254/Pdt.G/2006/Msy-TKN in the Takengon *shari'a* court, concerning the payment of *nafkah mut'ah* by a civil servant. The panel of judges, chaired by Chief Judge Hurriyah Abubakar, determined that compensation would be paid to the wife at one-third of the husband's wages over three months.

---

22   Interview with Hamid Pulungan, high judge of the Aceh provincial *shari'a* court, in Banda Aceh, 16 July 2012.

23   Interview with Surya, vice chair of Jantho *shari'a* court, in Aceh Besar, 25 April 2012.

24   Interview with Surya, vice chair of Jantho *shari'a* court, in Aceh Besar, 25 April 2012.

It is clear that the judges in the case of the civil servant divorce plaintiff did not refer to PP No. 10/1983 or PP No. 45/1990 in determining the payment methods and amount of payment due.[25] When this rule is implemented, it would seem that judges prefer not to implement the government regulations but rather choose fiqh arguments, which they consider more beneficial and fairer. The Supreme Court recommended against referring to PP No. 10/1983, and PP No. 45/1990 in determining a divorce case. Thus, where there is legal uncertainty, the judges are tasked with using *ijtihad*, or their own legal reasoning, to reach a just decision.

Implementation of the Divorce Payment Decision

According to the deputy chief judge of the Watansoppeng religious court, Abdul Salam, in the implementation of the divorce and the payment of the wife's *nafkah* there is a disparity of regulations that has led to family law in Indonesia not being enforced in a holistic way (Salam 2013: 1–7). This has led to wives feeling that there is a systematic injustice in law enforcement, at least with regard to divorce. This feeling is understandable, because under law rights and obligations should proceed in a parallel and balanced manner, as inseparable as two sides of a coin. However, while the rights to divorce and the husband's obligations are ideally governed by legislation, in reality this is not the case.

Judge Salam asserted that, as the intention of law enforcement is to fulfil the sense of justice, a solution must be found. Accordingly, in order to prevent further discrepancies and exemptions in the execution of the divorce agreement, the Supreme Court should promptly issue a regulation or circular to govern the implementation of divorce decisions regarding payments to the wife. This would ensure effective implementation of the decisions, to the satisfaction of the wife. In more concrete terms, the role of court registrars would need to be strengthened in implementing the decision, so that they can withhold issuing a divorce certificate until the terms of the judicial decision are fulfilled.

Further attention is required to overcome the lack of legal regulations binding the court and the husband's place of work to 'enforce' the payment of a portion of his wages to the ex-wife. Without a claim lodged by the ex-wife, the husband's place of work will not take the initiative to garnish his wages.[26] Simi-

---

25   Interview with Judge A. Karim Basyah at the Jantho *shari'a* court, in Aceh Besar, 2 May 2012.

26   Interview with plaintiff in a divorce case in the Jantho *shari'a* court, in Aceh Besar, 26 January 2013.

larly the government agency or higher education institution will not apportion part of his wages for his ex-wife, even though this is mandated by a government regulation. In one instance, even when the public service accounts section knew a staff member had divorced his wife, they did not share his wages with her, claiming there was no clear legal umbrella. The ex-wife did not report to her ex-husband's place of work, nor was there any initiative from the ex-husband's superiors to share the wages. The treasurer said, 'I am a low-ranking official; I only implement orders from my superiors'.[27]

The weakness of the legislation governing the authority of the judges in safeguarding the implementation of decisions was also indicated by Safwani [pseudonym], a lawyer and NGO activist in Lhokseumawe and Lhoksukon. He said that, although judges lack the authority to check and supervise the implementation of their decisions, judges still function as law enforcers in the community. He recalled many cases that violated the law regarding *nafkah* for children, where money was paid in full in the first month, only partially in the second month, and in the third month not at all.[28]

Hasyim (2006) explains that there are two strategies related to the payment of *nafkah* at the Jantho *shari'a* court (pp. 80–88). In cases where the divorce has been granted, if no money has been brought to pay the *nafkah* but there is joint property to be shared, the decision may be implemented, as happened in case No. 23/Pdt.G/2003/P-JTH. In this case the husband uttered the *talak* but did not pay the money, then the judge granted the divorce because the wife would obtain her half of the joint property, and thus she would enjoy economic security. In other cases, the implementation of a decision may be postponed if there is no joint property and no money brought to pay the *nafkah*, as happened in other divorce cases decided at the Jantho *shari'a* court.

Conclusion

Judges in Aceh consider the conduct of the two parties and the couple's economic situation when making judgments. Judges view the provision of *mut'ah* and *iddah* payments as a form of protection of women's rights, yet often these rights are not well implemented despite being regulated by Government Regulation No. 10/1983 (Ihsan, 2006, p. 85). If these payments are not made, this

---

27   Interview with a treasurer and paymaster in a higher education institution in Aceh Province, 2 December 2012.

28   Interview with Safwani, a lawyer, in Lhoksukon, 23 August 2013.

will strongly affect a woman's economic, social, and legal status. If she has children, she may be unable to guarantee them adequate and appropriate levels of education, nutrition, physical health, and financial stability. Nevertheless, implementation of Government Regulation No. 10/1983, concerning civil servants, is problematic when judges and even the Supreme Court consider it to be contrary to the principle of *fiqh* and Islamic law.

Based on the above study which focuses on several divorce cases including the civil servant who divorces his wife, it can be seen that in making their decisions, judges factor in the behavior of the wife: the better the wife's behaviour then the greater the amount of the subsistence payment. This is seen in the cases studied in both Banda Aceh and Jantho. Consideration of the wife's behaviour is more dominant than the ability of the husband to pay, although the ability of the husband is also one of the important considerations. Observing these facts, the legal reality is quite encouraging and deserves to be appreciated because judges, through the institution of the *shari'a* court, tend to protect women's rights, positioning women before the law with equality and fairness.

Bibliography

Abdurrahman. (2000). *Hareuta peunulang: Suatu penelitian di Kabupaten Pidie*. Banda Aceh, Indonesia: Pusat Penelitian Ilmu Sosial dan Budaya, Unsyiah.

Bowen, J.R. (2003). *Islam, law and equality in Indonesia: An anthropology of public reasoning*. Cambridge, England: Cambridge University Press.

Dahlan, A.A. (1996). *Ensiklopedi Hukum Islam* (Book II). Jakarta, Indonesia: Ichtiar Baru Van Hoeve.

Duriati, A.S. (2009). *Pelaksanaan putusan perceraian atas nafkah istri dan anak dalam Pengadilan Agama Semarang*. (Unpublished master's thesis). Diponegoro University, Semarang.

Ghazaly, A.R. (2006). *Fiqh munakahat*. Jakarta, Indonesia: Kencana.

Hasyim, A. (1993). Shari'a and codification: The Singapore experience. In S. Tebba (Ed.), *The latest development in Islamic law in Southeast Asia: Case study of family law and its codification* (p. 113). Bandung, Indonesia: Mizan.

Hasyim, A.M. (2006). *Eksekusi putusan cerai thalak dan kaitannya dengan gugatan rekonpensi: Studi kasus di Mahkamah Syar'iyyah Jantho* (Unpublished master's thesis). Syiah Kuala University, Banda Aceh.

Ihsan, M. (2006). *Pembayaran nafkah mut'ah istri dari suami PNS yang bercerai: Studi kasus di Mahkamah Syar'iyyah Takengon*. (Unpublished master's thesis). Banda Aceh: Universitas Syiah Kuala, Banda Aceh.

Mujieb, M.A. (1994). *Kamus istilah fiqih*. Jakarta, Indonesia: Pustaka Firdaus.

Muzdhar, A., & Nasution, K. (Eds). (2003). *Hukum Keluarga di dunia Islam modern: Studi perbandingan dan keberanjakan UU modern dari kitab-kitab fikih.* Jakarta, Indonesia: Ciputat Press.

Nuruddin, A., & Tarigan, A.A. (2004). *Hukum Perdata Islam di Indonesia: Studi kritis perkembangan Hukum Islam dari fikih, UU No. 1/1974 sampai KHI.* Jakarta, Indonesia: Kencana.

Salam, A. (2013). *Menimbang 'rasa keadilan' pada eksekusi talak atas putusan yang terdapat hak-hak isteri.* Retrieved from https://badilag.mahkamahagung.go.id/artikel-badilag.

Salim, A., Nurlaelawati, E., Marcoes, L., & Sayuti, W. (2009). *Demi keadilan dan kesetaraan: Dokumentasi program sensitivitas gender Hakim Agama.* Jakarta, Indonesia: PUSKUMHAM.

Salim, A. (2006). *Praktek penyelesaian formal dan informal masalah pertanahan, kewarisan dan perwalian pasca tsunami di Banda Aceh dan Aceh Besar.* Banda Aceh, Indonesia: International Development Law Organization.

Syahrizal. (2012). *Penetapan kadar nafkah iddah kepada isteri setelah terjadi perceraian: Studi kasus di Mahkamah Syar'iyyah Banda Aceh.* (Unpublished master's thesis). Faculty of Shari'a, IAIN Ar-Raniry, Banda Aceh.

Simanungkalit, R.MM. (2008). *Perceraian pasangan suami isteri bagi pemeluk agama Kristen: Studi kasus di wilayah hakim Pengadilan Negeri Yogyakarta.* Yogyakarta, Indonesia: Faculty of Law, Indonesia University.

Supriyadi, D., & Mustafa. (2009). *Perbandingan Hukum Perkawinan di Dunia Islam.* Bandung, Indonesia: Pustaka al-Fikris.

Syarifuddin, A. (2006). *Hukum Perkawinan Islam di Indonesia: Antara fiqih munakahat dan Undang-undang Perkawinan.* Jakarta, Indonesia: Kencana.

Zein, S.E.M. (2004). *Problematika Hukum Keluarga Islam Kontemporer: Analisis yuridis dengan pendekatan ushuliyah.* Jakarta, Indonesia: Kencana.

Laws and Regulations

Government Regulation No. 10 of 1983 on Permission for Marriage and Divorce for Civil Servants

Government Regulation No. 45 of 1990 on the Change of the Government Regulation No. 10 of 1983 on Permission for Marriage and Divorce for Civil Servants

Law No. 1 of 1974 on Marriage

Presidential Instructions No. 1 of 1991 on Compilation of Islamic Law

Ordinance of Marriages of Indonesian Christians in Java, Minahasa, and Ambon (Huwelijksordonnantie Christen-Indonesier Java, Minahasa, en Amboina, (Ord. 15 February 1993) S. 1933 No. 74).

Court Decisions

Jantho *shari'a* court Decision No. 39/Pdt.G/2012/MS-JTH (FL and FLN Case)
Banda Aceh *shari'a* court Decision No. 267/Pdt.G/2011/MS-Bna (TD and DS Case)

Court Cases

Jantho religious court Decision No. 23/Pdt.G/2003/PA-JTH
Takengon *shari'a* court Decision No. 254/Pdt.G/2006/Msy-TKN

CHAPTER 7

Disputing Marriage Payments in Indonesia
A Comparative Study of Aceh and South Sulawesi

Arskal Salim

Marriage payments in Middle Eastern and South Asian Muslim communities are often in the form of a contingent payment or yearly installments, or only given to the wife upon demand or divorce (Moors, 1994, 1995; Pearl & Menski, 1998). In contrast, marriage payments in many Indonesian Muslim circles are usually paid in full at the time of marriage. While disputes over marriage gifts in other Muslim countries are frequently related to and result in divorce, this kind of dispute is not common in Indonesia's religious courts. In various parts of Indonesia, such disputes may be part of divorce proceedings, but do not constitute an independent cause or key grounds for applying for divorce.

This chapter examines marriage payment disputes in two largely Muslim Indonesian provinces, Aceh and South Sulawesi, through comparative analysis of the practice and meaning of marriage payments. The nature of these marriage payment disputes, the legal processes and settlements in the religious courts, and the contribution of village elders deserve in-depth investigation and discussion. Most importantly, this chapter investigates why and how disputes arise over marriage payments in Indonesia. I analyze the notion of marriage payments and their varied forms, the multiple ways that different local actors understand them in relation to Islamic precepts and laws, and how marriage payment disputes are settled. Finally, I compare case studies in Aceh and South Sulawesi, and conclude that the courts in both regions consider evidence presented by the disputing parties and that court decisions do not appear to necessarily (dis)advantage one gender over the other.

Local Notion and Practice

Before delving further, it is important to clarify that marriage payments can constitute a variety of forms of gifts. Of these gifts, *mahr* or Islamic bridewealth is a key part of Islamic marriage ceremonies. Despite the lack of consensus among Muslim jurists as to whether *mahr* is required to legitimize the Islamic

© KONINKLIJKE BRILL NV, LEIDEN, 2019 | DOI:10.1163/9789004386297_009

marriage contract, marriage payments, including *mahr*, have been viewed as obligatory for marriage in many Muslim communities. For Muslims, *mahr* and other marriage payments not only constitute an important element of Islamic marriage but also have multiple social roles and functions.

In many Muslim social contexts, marriage gifts convey important meanings related to social status. In both Aceh and South Sulawesi, the ability to provide large marriage payments or gifts traditionally enables those of the upper class or aristocracy to demonstrate their distinct social status. Similarly, marriage gifts can 'establish' status for lower-class people, enabling them to attain a social status more equal to those in the upper social strata, despite the fact that they don't create true equality. In Aceh, the social rank of both the bride's and groom's family is a key consideration in determining the size of the marriage payment. The social class mobilization function of marriage payments is more evident in South Sulawesi. However, for many ordinary Muslims of different communities in Indonesia, the gift of a set of Islamic prayer equipment as *mahr* or bridewealth is quite popular and considered enough for a bride. This kind of marriage gift reflects modesty in marriage, which is thought to be an essence of Islamic moral values.

The difference in how marriage payments are perceived is related to local social structures. While in South Sulawesi social status and hierarchy remain important, in Aceh the social strata have greatly changed and social interaction seems to be on a more equal footing, which has somewhat affected the form of marriage payment paid or delivered to a bride. However, this neither means that Aceh is a classless society nor that the amounts of marriage payments are less in Aceh than in South Sulawesi.

Aceh

In Aceh, *mahr* marriage payments usually take the form of gold, although they may also be paid in an equivalent amount of rupiah. Aceh's gold marriage payment is measured in a unit known locally as *mayam*, with each *mayam* being equal to 3.3 grams of gold (in late 2017, equivalent to USD135). The minimum marriage payment in Aceh is three *mayam* of gold, which may take the form of gold jewellery or gold coins. Some brides may receive five, six, or ten *mayam* of gold as their *mahr*. The general practice is that the *mahr* given to a bride should not be less than that received by her elder sister or her mother (Syah, 1974). Acehnese women with an upper-class background may expect to receive a far more bridewealth, exceeding (and sometimes greatly exceeding) ten *mayam*. In recent years more *mayam* has commonly been given to brides. In Krueng Mane, in the North Aceh district, brides have been given 15 to 30 *mayam* and even as much as 50 *mayam* (Ayu, 2010).

DISPUTING MARRIAGE PAYMENTS IN INDONESIA

Practices may differ from one village to another. A woman from an upper-class family may still expect to receive a larger marriage payment than others. However, the aristocratic background of a family has never been the sole determinant of the amount of marriage payments. A bride's parents may demand more from the groom, sometime much more than the normal amount of marriage payments. This is especially true if the bride is very beautiful, has a higher education, or has rich parents.

For example, when the chairman of the Adat Council of North Aceh, Usman Budiman, married off his daughters, each of them received a bridewealth of 25 *mayam*. While Usman is not a *teuku* (an Acehnese aristocratic title), he was chairman of the North Aceh district legislature for almost 20 years during the Suharto regime. This position brought him and his family into the Acehnese social upper class. Despite this, if the families of his sons-in-law had sought to negotiate a marriage payment of less than 25 *mayam*, Usman said he would have been happy to accept the offer. However, the families felt that such negotiations would only humiliate them in the eyes of the community. They preferred instead to pay the quite sizeable amount of marriage payment requested by Usman to demonstrate their social worth. Similarly, when Usman married his only son to a nurse from a commoner background, he was ready to offer a marriage payment of up to 50 *mayam* to demonstrate his social status to the public. Yet his daughter-in-law's family only requested a set of Islamic prayer equipment as the bridewealth.

South Sulawesi

In South Sulawesi, especially among Bugis communities, the whole wedding process including the marriage payment is a key indication of one's social location (Miller, 1989). The local cultural notion of *siri* plays a role in this as well. As explained in more detail by the author of Chapter 2 of this volume, *siri* is closely related to concepts of dignity, self-esteem, pride, and honour. It motivates one to achieve higher status and better social rank. *Siri* helps regulate social interactions between individuals and families and the idealised positions they should adopt in South Sulawesi. The notion of *siri* is enshrined in all aspects of family life of the Bugis community, including marriage.

Marriage payments in Bugis communities consist of two types: (1) *sompa* or a symbolic sum of money given to the bride to indicate one's descent rank, and (2) *doi menre* or 'wedding expenses spending money' provided to the bride's family who will host the main wedding reception (Millar, 1989, p. 69). This second payment is intended to defray all costs related to catering, venue hire, and possibly also musical entertainment at the wedding reception. According to Millar (1989), *doi menre* is a volatile, showy, and aggressive indicator of status, while *sompa* is a passive and fixed indicator of status of the bride's descent rank (pp. 70–71). Both these types of marriage payment are considered to be a means for both the bride's and the groom's families to demonstrate their social rank, influence, and connections (Pelras, 1996, p. 159).

Although the amount may have changed greatly, the payment of *doi menre* still can be widely observed. As Millar (1989) writes, the general rule of this payment is that 'a woman may not receive a lesser marriage payment than her mother, but may receive more than her mother if her father's descent rank is higher than her mother's' (p. 30). This rule is also applicable due to the occasional government devaluation of the Indonesian currency. For instance, it is not uncommon for a mother who received Rp. 500,000 when she married in 1980, whilst her eldest daughter who married in 2004 received Rp. 15,000,000.

Being a symbolic token of the bride's descent rank, *sompa* was originally paid in gold coins. At the end of the nineteenth century, as noted by Pelras (1996), *sompa* was specified in units called 'kati' (pp. 156, 159–160). A bride from the highest rank could expect to receive up to 14 kati, while a bride from the lowest social rank would be happy to receive 1 kati or less. A kati was equivalent in value to 88 real or reyal, the minted currency of Portuguese Malacca, known and pronounced in South Sulawesi as *reyal*. These gold coins were the most likely currency given as *sompa* to Bugis noblewomen at that time (interview with Datu Andi Hasan Machmud, September 2012). Why this Portuguese Malaccan gold coin was preferred in marriage payments is unknown. Perhaps it was related to the meaning of the term '*real*' in Portuguese, namely royal or nobility. For, as Millar (1989) noted, a bride from a commoner background could not receive her marriage payment in kati or real, but only in ringgit (pp. 102–103). In addition, the amount received normally amounted to 11 ringgit or half a kati, and could not exceed 22 ringgit or one kati.

Marriage payment in the form of *sompa* in South Sulawesi has completely changed and taken various forms in the past few decades. According to Millar (1989), major changes in the monetary system several years after Indonesia's independence rendered the kati value of *sompa* insignificant (p. 103). *Sompa* thus became a purely symbolic mechanism for measuring status, given in set amounts corresponding to the descent rank of the bride. Currently, some brides from families who still consider themselves to be of noble descent will request *sompa* in the form of '88 real', to be mentioned at the wedding ceremony. In fact, even some commoners are now keen to have '88 real' declared as *sompa* before the wedding guests and noted on the marriage certificate.

How and in what ways the *sompa* of '88 real' is actually paid always varies. One way is to attach the *sompa* payment to a property. For instance, when a *sompa* is declared at a wedding, a statement immediately follows clarifying that the *sompa* resides in this or that rice field. So, the *sompa* of '88 real' has a shape and form, which could be a rice field or fruit trees. Today, it may also take the form of a house, money, or even company shares. According to the chief judge of the Makassar religious high court, quite frequently the bride or her close relatives do not pay particular attention to the form in which the *sompa* of '88 real' is presented. What concerns them more is that the groom should declare a gift of *sompa* to the bride in the form of valuable property, signalling the high social status of the bride's family. Although the *sompa* property belongs to the wife, it is often controlled by her husband and his family, especially if it is a rice field. Should the couple divorce, disputes may arise over who is more entitled to claim ownership of this *sompa* property.

Disputes over Marriage Payments

For some communities in Aceh and South Sulawesi, marriage payments are not just about bridewealth or a wedding ceremony; they are in fact linked to the bigger picture of a hierarchical society and the survival of this tradition. With this in mind, disputes over marriage payments undoubtedly entail espousal of, as well as challenges against, cultural values and the existing social order. To achieve their objectives, supporters and their opponents on both sides have employed social discourse and legal means. The following sections not only demonstrate how and why these material transactions turn into disputes but also discuss how marriage payments have been disputed in different forums.

Court disputes over marriage payments take place more often in South Sulawesi than in Aceh. This has largely to do with the fact that Bugis and Makassar communities have been more hierarchical societies than Aceh. In South Sulawesi, the social locations of both the bride's and groom's families are usually at stake when it comes to wedding ceremonies. In addition, marriage payments presented in the form of certificates of land ownership often lead to complications because court-based settlement of land property disputes requires authentic and accurate evidence presented to the judges. In contrast, in Aceh Islamic bridewealth or *mahr* is mostly paid in the form of gold jewellery. Given its portability, once a husband gives the gold objects to his wife, this bridewealth instantly enters the wife's possession, and marriage payments are thus not often disputed in Aceh's courtrooms. The gift of gold jewellery to the bride is straightforward and relatively trouble free.

The question of which marriage payment serves as Islamic bridewealth is often vague in South Sulawesi. While the *mayam* gold paid to the bride in Aceh is widely regarded as Islamic bridewealth there, there is no consensus in South Sulawesi whether the *sompa* functions as Islamic bridewealth. Pelras (1996) explains that what could be considered Islamic bridewealth or *mahr* in Bugis communities is not *sompa*, but *lise kawing* ('wedding substance'), which is usually a small sum of money (p. 156). Nowadays, *lise kawing* sometimes also takes the form of a printed copy of the Qur'an or a set of prayer equipment. However, Millar does not concur with Pelras's view. Millar (1989) notes that both *sompa* and *doi menre* were originally customary marriage payments, and although she observed that *sompa* was frequently announced and paid at Islamic marriage ceremonies, she does not conclude that both *sompa* and *doi menre* are identical to *mahr* in the Islamic marriage tradition (p. 70).

In relation to Millar's contention, one may wonder whether *sompa* has been given an Islamic identity, and, thus, been Islamized through the practice of marriage payments within Muslim communities in South Sulawesi over time. However, when we examine *sompa* as Islamic bridewealth in Bugis Muslim communities in South Sulawesi, informants offer different understandings of what constitutes *mahr* in Islamic marriage. There are three reasons for these varied interpretations of the function of *sompa*. The first is a lack of agreement over whether *sompa* is an Islamic form of *mahr*. Some informants considered *sompa* to be identical to *mahr*, but others said that *sompa* is a customary marriage gift to a bride. The second reason is the form of *sompa* given to a bride. If *sompa* takes the form of gold jewellery or gold coins of a specific size and weight, it is commonly viewed as the sort of *mahr* that a bride would possess. Yet, if *sompa* takes the symbolic form of '88 real' and it is linked to a land parcel or rice field, it is harder to interpret it as the typical kind of *mahr*. This is in part because such *sompa* is less concrete in nature due to the third reason, which is that a gift of land is often not noted on the marriage certificate. People automatically consider a payment to be *mahr* when it is stated on the marriage certificate. However, often *sompa* is not listed in the marriage certificate, especially if it takes the form of land. The space in the marriage certificate is too limited to detail the dimensions and location of a land parcel, if it is given to a bride as *mahr*. Due to this complexity and other reasons, disputes over marriage payments commonly emerge alongside divorce petitions filed at South Sulawesi's religious courts.

In Aceh, the difference between *mahr* as Islamic bridewealth and other forms of gifts presented to the bride upon her marriage is quite evident. Other than *mahr*, which usually takes the form of gold *mayam*, the bride in some districts of Aceh, Pidie district in particular, often receives unmovable gifts, such as a house, a land parcel, or a farm, from her parents. Such gifts are called 'peunulang' and continue to belong to the bride should divorce take place.

DISPUTING MARRIAGE PAYMENTS IN INDONESIA 133

However, if the bride dies and there are no surviving offspring, the groom will receive a half of this property as his inheritance share.

Has *mahr* ever been disputed in Aceh's *shari'a* courts? As explained by Fitriyel Hanif, an Islamic judge of Lhokseumawe *shari'a* court, marriage payment disputes in Aceh are not merely about bridewealth. Rather, disputes examined by Aceh's *shari'a* courts often relate to pre-marriage arrangements, usually in the form of oral prenuptial agreements stipulating gifts. According to Judge Hanif, this kind of dispute tends to arise from the wife's claim that her husband has failed to fulfil a promise or an agreement made orally before the marriage. Normally, such claims come up either after the wedding has taken place or after the couple has consummated the marriage. However, since the promised gift to the bride was not specified on the marriage certificate, the formal written requirement of lawful Islamic bridewealth was not met. As marriage certificates do not specify *mahr*, when husbands do not deliver marriage payments, wives may appear at court and demanded the promised gifts or payments from their husbands. This issue of marriage payments that do not materialize will be discussed in the following section.

Claiming Unpaid Payments

Wives' claims of unpaid bridewealth are frequently included in their petitions for divorce. In Aceh, this kind of dispute is often easily resolved, and many claims are settled without much judicial interference. Decision 65/2007 of the *shari'a* court of Lhokseumawe demonstrates how a divorcing couple agreed to quickly settle their dispute over unpaid *mahr*. Judge Fitriyel Hanif of Lhokseumawe *shari'a* court stated that such a dispute seldom reaches the courtroom, and is normally settled in the mediation room with the help of a mediator.

Nevertheless, a claim over marriage payments may emerge at court alongside the divorce application. This occurs when the wife, for one reason or another, submits a petition of divorce to the court whilst her husband has not yet provided full payment of *mahr* (the set amount of *mayam*). In another case, a wife received the bridewealth in full but then her husband borrowed it to start a new small business. Upon the collapse of his business, he was unable to return the *mahr* to his wife. Should a couple later seek divorce, the wife usually requests the husband to return the borrowed *mahr* or to pay the outstanding *mahr*.

To illustrate how unpaid marriage payments are disputed, Judge Hanif described a number of cases that reached the courtroom:

1. A woman consented to be the second wife of a successful businessman under the condition that, among others, her prospective husband would pay her Rp. 5,000,000 every month for maintenance and living costs (*nafkah*). The man agreed and paid the woman the stated amount. However, this payment was only paid for the first five months of the marriage. From the sixth months onwards, the husband failed to pay his second wife the set maintenance. When the case was brought to court, the wife asked the husband to pay all her outstanding *nafkah*. The judges accepted her claim since the husband admitted that he had made such a promise, and ordered him to pay the money due.

2. A man promised a woman that he would bring all his personal property (*harta bawaan*) into their joint marital property (*harta bersama*) should she agree to marry him. The woman agreed to marry the man under these terms. However, after a few years had passed, the husband still had not transferred his personal property. When there was a communication breakdown that destroyed their marriage, the wife filed a divorce petition to the court. In it, she included a claim for the husband's personal property on the grounds that it was part of the prenuptial agreement. The judges, however, did not accept her claim for two reasons: the husband denied the promise to transfer his personal property and the wife was not able to provide adequate evidence to support her claim.

3. A man offered a parcel of land to a woman should she agree to marry him. The land was still in the possession of the man's father who was already 80 years old. The husband told the wife that the land transfer would take place when they were officially married, as he expected his father would pass away soon. The man was sure that he would inherit this land since he was the only child still living in town (Lhokseumawe), all his siblings having moved to other cities, such as Jakarta, Medan, and Banda Aceh. However, 10 years after the wedding, the man's father was still living and the land had not been transferred. In addition, married relations between the couple had worsened since the husband wanted to marry another woman as his second wife. As the first wife did not agree to her husband taking another wife, her husband sought to divorce her. When this case came to court, the woman claimed that her husband should fulfil his promise to give her the parcel as previously agreed. Despite adequate evidence presented by the woman, the judges did not accept her claim because the land remained the property of the husband's father who was still alive. The judges found that the husband's pre-marital promise was unlawful because the land parcel to be granted was in the possession of another person.

DISPUTING MARRIAGE PAYMENTS IN INDONESIA

It appears from the above cases that the judges tend to accept claims of unpaid marriage payments provided there is adequate supporting evidence. In cases of unpaid marriage payments, the wife is not required to present evidence to support her claim. According to Judge Hanif, should the husband confirm the claim and express his willingness to repay all outstanding payments, the case is then resolved. For Judge Hanif, the husband's acknowledgement alone constitutes sufficient evidence to warrant acceptance of the wife's claim in marital property disputes. However, should the husband contest the wife's claim, she must provide convincing evidence, such as a written legal document or the testimony of witnesses. The following case demonstrates how a claim for marriage payments was granted based on the husband's acknowledgement alone.

Akbar vs. Erlita

This case was initiated when Akbar [pseudonym] submitted a divorce application to the Lhokseumawe *shari'a* court in March 2007. He wanted to divorce his wife, Erlita [pseudonym], because he claimed she was having an affair with another man and therefore did not serve as a good wife. Erlita argued that her husband had not been able to fulfil her sexual needs after three months of marriage. Concerning Akbar's application for divorce, Erlita did not have any objection provided Akbar agree to her claim over a number of marriage payments. These included unpaid *mahr* (5 gold *mayam*), unpaid *nafkah* (monthly maintenance) for the past four months, *iddah* (waiting period) monies, *muth'ah* divorce compensation fees, and *kiswah* (clothing) settlement, which came to over Rp. 14,000,000. Akbar did not refute any of his wife's claims. In fact, he settled payment of the overdue *mahr* and four months of *nafkah* while the divorce case was still being examined. As the judges determined there was no possible way to reconcile the couple, they granted Akbar permission to divorce his wife.

While dispute settlements of marriage payments in Aceh's courtrooms do not require evidence, as the above case shows, religious courts of South Sulawesi seem to require evidence and long hearings when examining these cases. A case from the Makassar religious court below is a good example of how the judges pay particular attention to local culture and focus carefully on each piece of evidence presented by the litigants.

Edi vs. Sari

Edi and Sari [pseudonyms] were married on 19 October 2009. Less than two years later, the husband lodged a divorce application on the grounds that his wife had been disrespectful and disobedient to him. This was because Sari had refused her husband's request to leave her parents' house and live with her husband in a separate house. In November 2010, a year after the marriage, Edi left his in-law's house.

The couple appeared in court for the first hearing in February 2011. Sari denied all allegations made against her. She countered that Edi had lied and told the court false stories. In fact, as a faithful wife, she had showed respect and great attention to her husband, even helping him look for a decent job. Further, through her father's connections, her husband had been finally able to find a good position with a big income at a private company. Sari regarded her husband as an ungrateful person who was ill mannered and acted in the manner described in the Indonesian aphorism '*air susu dibalas air tuba; habis manis sepah dibuang*', which roughly equates to a being a 'fair weather friend'.

For this reason, Sari made a counterclaim that upon divorce her husband should pay *muth'ah*, *nafkah maskan* (accommodation), and *kiswah* settlements for three months during the waiting period following divorce, and monthly child maintenance until their two-and-a-half-year-old daughter became an adult. In total, the claim came to Rp. 100,000,000. In addition, Sari asked her husband to surrender to her the unpaid *mahr*, namely a house located in Makassar. She claimed she had been given the house and that this was recorded on the marriage certificate.

Judge Syahidal chaired the panel of judges who examined this case. In an interview, Judge Syahidal explained that often the evidence is unclear in a dispute over land that constitutes a marriage payment. This is because the land's size and location are unspecified in the marriage certificate. For this reason, he paid close attention to the witnesses and evidence presented by both parties, including the religious official who recorded the couple's marriage. Considering all the information and evidence presented on the issue in question, Judge Syahidal and his two fellow judges summed up the legal facts as follows: Firstly, in one of the pre-wedding meetings, the families of the bride and the groom discussed the bridewealth. Both sides had agreed upon *mahr* in the form of a set of gold jewellery but the bride's family requested additional *mahr* in the form of a house. The groom's family, however, refused to grant the request for the house and threatened to cancel the wedding plans should the bride's family persist with their request.

Secondly, many relatives of the bride's family had been given to understand that a house would be provided as *mahr* for this marriage, although this was not the case. Thus, the bride's parents sought to save face by asking the groom's family to agree that a house would be announced as *mahr* at the marriage solemnization, despite the fact it was a fake declaration. For the bride's parents,

DISPUTING MARRIAGE PAYMENTS IN INDONESIA 137

this was mostly intended to let the guests and relatives who had come to the wedding ceremony know the great value of the bridewealth that was being given to their daughter.

Thirdly, the groom's parents agreed to this request to announce a house as *mahr* at the marriage solemnization. They understood this was to be done solely for the purpose of preventing shame from falling upon the bride's parents. For this reason, the marriage certificate did not record a house as *mahr* but only a set of gold jewellery as earlier agreed.

Finally, about a month after the wedding, the bride and her mother, without informing the groom, went to see the imam who had organized and recorded the marriage ceremony. They asked him to add a house to the bridewealth by recording it on the marriage certificate. The imam did not fulfil this request. When the groom discovered they both had requested this, he complained and reported to the police that a criminal offence had been committed, namely attempted forgery of information on the marriage certificate.

The judges considered the imam's testimony to be crucial evidence in resolving the case. As the official marriage registrar, the imam has full authority and responsibility for recording the *mahr* on the certificates of Muslim marriages. His testimony before the court is worth elaborating here to see how the judges decided the case. Under oath, the imam was reported to have said:

> The bridewealth was a set of gold jewellery and a house. They were both mentioned during the solemnization of marriage, but I didn't record the house on the marriage certificate because relevant property documents had not been handed [to the bride]. What had been offered was a set of gold jewellery. I did not see the groom's family submit a house key as the bride's *mahr*. When I asked for the property document, the groom's family replied that the document was being processed. Nonetheless, a month after the wedding, the bride and her mother came to my house showing an agreement between the two families on the approved *mahr* from a pre-wedding meeting and asked me to add a house as the bride's *mahr* to the marriage certificate. [He did not do so.] A year after the marriage, the groom's family visited my house three times questioning my role in adding a house as *mahr* to the marriage certificate. Thus, I wrote a statement explaining that I had not added it [to the marriage certificate] since there were no facts or authentic documents that supported [the provision of] a house as *mahr*. [In fact], no additional notation of a house as *mahr* was made in the marriage minutes.

Having closely analyzed all the evidence presented, including the testimony of witnesses, the judges concluded that the bride's *mahr* did not include a house. The agreement to include a house as *mahr* made in the pre-wedding meeting was, they found, more of a cultural arrangement than a legal contract. The judges considered this kind of agreement to be flawed and lacking validity to support the bride's entitlement to a house. The panel of judges were further convinced of their decision because the marriage certificate did not record a house as a *mahr* during the solemnization of marriage. Instead, the house was suspiciously incorporated into the existing *mahr* one month after the wedding by the wife and her mother. The addition of the house as *mahr* to the marriage certificate was unknown by the *imam* who had the sole authority to make any changes in the certificate.

Returning Marriage Payments

Part of the reason why marriage payments are frequently disputed is due to their special position in Islamic marriage. Teungku Muhammad Isa, the deputy chairman of the Lhokseumawe Ulama Consultative Council (MPU), explained that *mahr* is not an essential element of the marriage. The solemnization of marriage (*akad nikah*) is valid even without *mahr* being mentioned. However, the reason why *mahr* is considered compulsory and something that must be presented to the bride is because the groom wants to consummate the marriage. He said:

> Even though *mahr* is not mentioned in the marriage solemnization, the marriage remains valid. This has to do with the fact that *mahr* is compulsory not because of the marriage itself, *mahr* being neither a requirement nor a pillar of the marriage. Rather, *mahr* is necessary due to sexual intercourse.
>
> Interview on 8 August 2011

If the bride receives *mahr* in full, what happens if divorce takes place before the marriage has been consummated? Will the *mahr* be returned? According to the chairman of the MPU, Teungku Asnawi, in this situation it is obligatory for the bride to return half of the paid *mahr* to the groom. Why is it only half? Teungku Asnawi further explained that, 'when a marriage has been solemnized, repayment of half of *mahr* is compulsory. This is because solemnization of the marriage changes the status of the woman from virgin (*perawan*) to widow (*janda*) should her new husband divorce her immediately after the wedding, even if the marriage is never consummated'. This means that half the paid *mahr* is for the solemnization of marriage, while the other half acknowledges the sexual access. In the view of Teungku Asnawi, this notion of returning half the paid *mahr* is based on *shari'a*, and Shafi'i jurisprudence in particular, and is a common practice in Aceh.

Non-returnable Marriage Payments

In South Sulawesi, different practices are followed for repayment of *mahr* to the groom depending on whether the marriage has been consummated (*ba'da al-dukhul*) or unconsummated (*qabla al-dukhul*). In Bugis communities if the marriage is unconsummated *mahr* is not returned to the groom, however, in certain Makassar ethnic communities the paid *mahr* should be returned.

As mentioned earlier, *mahr* or Islamic bridewealth and other marriage payments often overlap in South Sulawesi. In fact, it is unclear whether *sompa* can be identified or function as Islamic bridewealth. This is the source of the emerging disputes over marriage payments in South Sulawesi, including cases where the husband requests return of part of the marriage payments from his former wife upon divorce. This especially applies for husbands whose wives provide no sexual access at all. The question is: what kind of marriage payments should an ex-husband request return of: *mahr, sompa, pabbere'* (wedding gifts), or *doi menre* (wedding expenses payment)?

In her research on women, sex, and marriage in Sidrap, South Sulawesi, Idrus (2003) discovered different practices of returning marriage payments (pp. 240–241). Despite the stipulation in the *Lontara'* (Bugis palm-leaf manuscripts that record knowledge on such topics as history, science, custom, and laws) that half the *sompa* and all wedding gifts must be returned if the marriage is unconsummated, it is uncommon in Sidrap for the groom's parents to ask the bride's family to return those marriage payments. What often happens though is that the groom's family requests the return of the wedding expenses payment, but rarely are such payments returned. For the bride's family, this latter payment is customarily considered a non-returnable item. This concept is locally known as '*nanre api*' or burnt by fire, which means that all the money was fully spent on wedding-related expenses, including catering, hire of venue, hire of traditional marriage costumes for the bride and groom, and much more (Farida Patitinggi, interview 28 July 2011).

Asril vs. Armelia

A case of (non-)returnable marriage payments from the Sungguminasa religious court is worth mentioning here. Asril, 28 years [pseudonym] proposed Armelia, 20 years [pseudonym] in mid-2010. While Armelia was not interested in marrying him, her parents welcomed Asril and forced Armelia to marry him. The bridewealth included three gold rings, a gold necklace, and a wedding expenses payment of Rp. 50,000,000. Armelia was not happily married and never allowed Asril to touch her. In fact, five days after the wedding, Armelia left her husband and returned to live at her parents' house. More than three months later, Armelia submitted a petition of divorce to the Sungguminasa religious court on the grounds that she had been physically abused. Asril denied this allegation, but was willing to divorce Armelia should she return all the bridewealth, not only the *mahr* but also the wedding expenses payment.

As the judges found no evidence of physical abuse, they did not accept Armelia's divorce petition. Instead, the judges accepted the husband's counterclaim by granting a *khuluk* divorce (divorce at the request of the wife who pays compensation) and sentenced the Armelia to return all marriage payments, including the wedding expenses payment. The reasons given included: (1) to restore justice within society, (2) to remedy the ex-husband's psychological wounds, and (3) to provide an example for future forced marriages.[1]

The plaintiff, Armelia, was not content with the decision of the Sungguminasa religious court and therefore lodged an appeal with the high religious court of Makassar. The appellate judge panel that examined the case consisted of the panel chair and two panel members. The decision of this appellate judge panel was to rescind the judgment of the lower religious court. Yet, this was not a unanimous decision, as one member of the panel dissented.

Chief Judge Zainab and Judge Anwar believed that since the marriage collapsed soon after the wedding and there was no possibility of reconciliation, the plaintiff's divorce petition could be accepted without considering it a *khulu'* application. Both judges noted that, since from the very beginning the plaintiff had not sought to marry the defendant, thus the goal of marriage (to achieve a harmonious and loving family) was unlikely to be achieved. It was better for the marriage to end than lead to quarrels and protracted fights between the couple.

Regarding the plaintiff's obligation to return the wedding expenses payment, the two judges referred to the Bugis custom that repayment of the wedding expenses spent rarely occurs, unless it has been pre-agreed between the

---

1 See Decision of the Sungguminasa religious court No. 437/2010.

DISPUTING MARRIAGE PAYMENTS IN INDONESIA 141

bride's and groom's families. Both judges also drew on the customary concept of *nanre api* to reject the husband's counterclaim. These two judges maintained that the guests of the two families had benefited from the wedding expenses payment during the wedding celebration.[2]

While the two judges agreed to take the local custom *nanre api* into account to justify a non-returnable wedding expenses payment, the dissenting judge, Judge Samparaja, chose to support the lower court's decision which he found just. Concurring with the Sungguminasa religious court's decision, Judge Samparaja added two items of legal reasoning from different sources to warrant repayment upon *khulu'*. He quoted the Prophet's saying in the case of Thabit b. Qais b. Shammas, who accepted the return of *mahr* (in the form of a farm) from his wife so as to divorce her. The wife was not happily married and told the Prophet, 'I do not criticize his behaviour or piety, nor do I want to disobey any Islamic doctrine'. The Prophet replied, 'Would you return the farm he gave you?' The wife answered, 'I would'. Then the Prophet said to Thabit, 'Kindly accept the farm back and declare a single divorce [*talak satu*] upon her, in that way you have kindly released her'.

Judge Samparaja also cited the statement of Sayid Sabiq, as written in his well-known book, *Fiqh al-Sunna*:

> That a husband accepts a *khulu'* [compensation from his wife] is considered just and appropriate because when he has given [the wife] a *mahr*, paid all marriage expenses, the wedding reception and been encumbered to provide her maintenance, suddenly the wife in return rebels and asks for divorce. [In this case,] it is thus just that the wife should return all she has received.

In the view of Judge Samparaja, the repayment should help remedy, albeit only slightly, the husband's deep disappointment or his resentment, and would render him able to sincerely let the wife go. Judge Samparaja's contention that the case must be resolved through *khulu'* was perhaps motivated by his suspicion that the bride's parents sought to justify requesting a high amount of spending money, which was unlikely be returned because of the *nanre api* custom. Assuming this may have occurred, Judge Samparaja found the decision of the Sungguminasa religious court to apply *khulu'* in this case was correct. Apparently, he believed that judges should invent and create law based on cases examined. He stated, '[A]s an agent of change, a judge should not disregard this

---

2 See the appeal decision of the Makassar religious high court No. 78 of 2011.

and in fact should have the law function as a tool of social engineering. The law is there to protect human interests. It is created and produced to encourage social change so as to amend some social practices, which are inimical to the sense of justice within society'.

Despite this dissenting opinion, the final decision of the Makassar high religious court was to revoke the judgment of the Sungguminasa religious court, and the divorce petition submitted by the plaintiff was thus accepted. The decision of the high religious court was achieved through majority vote, in which two judges concurred and one judge dissented. Thus no order to repay the wedding expenses payment to the groom was included into the appeal decision.

Returnable Marriage Payments

In some Makassar ethnic communities, the return of bridewealth to the groom can still take place even after consummation of the marriage. This practice takes place especially among the people of Julubori, a small village in the district of Gowa. In this village, bridewealth is locally known as 'sunrang', which is quite similar to *sompa*. The difference is that most *sunrang* in this village is presented in the form of land, such as a farm, a rice field, or a house. During the marriage ceremony the people of Julubori feel more proud if they can mention land as *mahr* rather than gold. If a groom or his family possesses land and is reluctant to present it to his bride as *sunrang*, the villagers would consider this shameful (*siri*). For this reason, the groom always announces a land parcel as the bridewealth even if he does not own one or have the right to give it away, despite the strong likelihood this will lead to disputes. Such disputes can be settled within the extended family or with the help of the village elders. It is unknown whether any dispute over marriage payments from this village has ever reached the courtroom.

The practice in Julubori shows that these types of marriage payments are returned when divorce takes place. Interestingly, *sunrang* is returned to the husband or his family, but not because the marriage has not been consummated. The *sunrang* is returned mostly if the couple is childless. One of the village elders, Abdul Rajab, related his experience regarding this practice. His daughter married a local man, and she received a *sunrang* in the form of three hectares of land. However, their marriage did not last long. Once divorce took place, his daughter returned the land to the husband. The daughter felt ashamed to retain the *sunrang* since no children had been born from the marriage.

DISPUTING MARRIAGE PAYMENTS IN INDONESIA

A local imam named Sirua confirmed Rajab's account. As imam, Sirua officially assists the sub-district religious office in organizing and recording marriages that take place in Julubori. In his view, *sunrang* as practiced in Julubori is equal to *mahr* in Islam. For the past 10 years, Sirua has recorded the *sunrang* presented to the bride as *mahr*, and written it down on the marriage certificate. However, he would not let a wife retain the *sunrang* after a husband divorced her, when the marriage had been consummated and the couple had no children. According to him and many other elders in the village, although this practice contradicts Islamic teaching, where the woman should have full control over her *mahr*, this is what has been practiced in Julubori for a very long time. The village head, Anshar, confirmed that the practice of returning *sunrang* or *mahr* to the husband upon divorce is the local custom, whereas *sunrang* is retained by the wife if the couple have a child. The village head understood that if such a case were brought to the religious court, the ex-wife would win and retain the *sunrang*, but he was unsure that anyone from his village would be brave enough to violate this custom, lest they be regarded as an outsider. Anshar said, 'This practice has a long pedigree in the tradition of our ancestors. It would be bizarre for anyone to contravene this practice'.

Apparently, the notion of *sunrang* in Julubori is not simply a gift or bridewealth for the bride. Instead, it is given to the wife to be later transferred to the couple's child or children. When the couple has a child, the ownership of the *sunrang* will shift from the mother to the child; as one of Julubori village elders said, '*Sunrang* is actually a property to be transferred to children through their mothers'. Thus, if the couple divorces childless then *sunrang* should be returned. In this situation it is often the wife's father, rather than his daughter, who is more motivated to return the property to his former son-in-law. This is to prevent his feeling *siri* should the *sunrang* be retained. Rajab acknowledged that his daughter had no child from her marriage, so he would have been ashamed if he did not return the *sunrang*. In addition, according to Julubori village elders, should a parent in such a case retain the *sunrang*, the social consequences for him and his wife would be manifold: they would not be able to marry off their children in the future, their social status would suffer, and people would talk about them behind their backs.

The practice of returning marriage payments in Julubori village has no comparable cases in Aceh. Despite this, it is probably interesting to contrast the *sunrang* in Julubori with the practice of *peunulang* in Aceh Besar and Pidie. Both *sunrang* and *peunulang* are a kind of gift offered to the bride upon marriage. However, while *peunulang* is given by the bride's father to his daughter and will remain hers even if divorce takes place, *sunrang* is offered to the bride by the groom or his parents and must be returned upon divorce should the marriage be childless.

Conclusion

Unlike disputes over marriage payments in Muslim Middle Eastern contexts that mostly centre on the protection of wives against financial ruin in the aftermath of divorce, similar disputes in Aceh and South Sulawesi are more about restoration of social dignity. Some disputes were indeed economically motivated, mostly initiated by the husband to ask for the return of the marriage payment in full or part. Although these appear on the surface to be financial matters, social dignity often underpins such divorce petitions to the courts.

Most disputes over marriage payments were settled without difficulty thanks to the evidence presented before the judges, which include the marriage certificate, the husband's testimony, the testimony of the marriage registrar, and so on. These help shape the judges' conclusions, enabling them to make a final decision by referring to various applicable norms, including Islamic legal jurisprudence, the Indonesian *Compilation of Islamic Law*, and existing customary laws. It is worth noting here that cases discussed in this chapter do not show that gender determines the final outcome in court. Wives who bring a lawsuit before the court must support their claims with valid evidence. Making strong claims without adequate evidence will not guarantee that the judges will accept the wives' claims solely based on gender-related affirmative actions.

Bibliography

Ayu, R. (2010). *Makna mahar (jeulamee) dalam penghargaan keluarga istri pada sistem perkawinan suku Aceh: Studi deskriptif di Krueng Mane Kecamatan Muara Batu Aceh Utara*. (Unpublished final year paper) Universitas Sumatera Utara, Medan.

Idrus, N.I. (2003). *To take each other: Bugis practices of gender, sexuality and marriage* (Unpublished doctoral dissertation). The Australian National University, Canberra. Retrieved from https://openresearch-repository.anu.edu.au/bitstream/1885/47288/6/02whole.pdf.

Millar, S.B. (1989). *Bugis weddings: Ritual of social location in modern Indonesia*. (Monograph Series, No. 29). Berkeley, CA: Center for South and Southeast Asian Studies, University of California.

Moors, A. (1994). Women and dower property in twentieth-century Palestine: The case of Jabal Nablus. *Islamic Law and Society 1* (3), 301–331.

Moors, A. (1995). *Women, property and Islam: Palestinian experiences 1920–1990.* Cambridge, England: Cambridge University Press.

Pearl, D., & Menski, W. (1998). *Muslim family law.* London: Sweet & Maxwell.

Pelras, C. (1996). *The Bugis.* Cambridge, England: Blackwell Publishers.

Syah, I.M. (1974). *Adat perkawinan di Aceh Utara.* Banda Aceh, Indonesia: Pusat Latihan Penelitian Ilmu-Ilmu Sosial.

Laws and Regulations

Presidential Instructions No. 1 of 1991 on Compilation of Islamic Law

Court Decisions

Lhokseumawe *shari'a* court Decision No. 65/Pdt.G/2007/MS-Lhok
Sungguminasa religious court Decision No. 437/Pdt.G/2010/PA-Sgm
Makassar high religious court Decision No. 78/Pdt.G/2011/PTA-Mks

Epilogue

John R. Bowen

The chapters of this volume allow us to better understand the ways in which Indonesian women and men engage in strategies to secure rights to property in Islamic legal settings. Now well into the 21st century, we can begin to ask how the national political and legal changes that took place after the fall of former president Suharto in 1998 have reshaped the social field on the local level. Major changes include the restructuring of the court system, the decentralization of many powers to the district and local levels, and the growth of organized challenges in the name of Islam to the Constitutional Court. In addition, some judges work in regional environments where they face challenges to state Islamic rules.

On the national level the main legal narrative has been one of incorporating Islam into a unified system of state law. As with most other Muslim-majority societies in the world, Indonesia has selected, from among the vast corpus of rules and principles that make up fiqh, certain rules to be enforced through statute, decree, and court decisions, or in less formalized ways, for example through informal instructions within a ministry. This process of 'statifying' Islam at times places the state in opposition to Islamic bodies over particular interpretations of Islam. Since 1998 Indonesia has seen a florescence of government agencies giving legal enforceability to particular interpretations of Islamic rules, from the Constitutional Court down to the edicts of districts and cities concerning immoral behaviour. The state also has sought to increase the extent to which it directly regulates some religious practices, such as the collection of *zakat* (the annual tithe). Islam is more thoroughly statified than ever before.

At the same time, however, conflicts have escalated over the role of the state in enforcing tenets of Islam. These conflicts may be signs of a healthy constitutional politics, as are the differences of view over what is often termed 'the balance of liberty and piety'. But in other cases, the state has retreated in the face of illegal acts, as in the case of sometimes-murderous attacks against Ahmadiyya mosques and against churches, at times under the cover of allegations that the mosques and churches 'violated regulations'. Successive presidents have chosen not to challenge the vigilantism of the Islamic Defence Front (Front Pembela Islam). Although Indonesia's leaders rightly argue that democracy protects freedom of expression, they are not consistently vigilant in protecting religious expression.

EPILOGUE

We can thus say that 'shari'a in Indonesia is mostly a state matter', insofar as legally enforced elements of *shari'a* are, by definition, part of positive law and thus enacted by the state. The chapters in this volume document this claim, but they do so from the standpoint of Indonesian women and men who pursue their own strategies to secure their rights to wealth through legal means. We can also understand *shari'a* in a way that includes prayer, birth and death rituals, and so forth, and there the state plays at most a minor role. So, the process in question is that whereby 'shari'a' comes to be identified with 'Islamic law', or positive law.

The statifying of Islam in Indonesia does not necessarily mean greater uniformity in legal practices, because as political bodies have multiplied and secured new powers since 1998, so the possibilities for conflicts have increased, both between state bodies and vis-à-vis non-state elements. For example, Aceh's special status, which allows its parliament to enact laws based on *shari'a*, contains a critical ambiguity as to the degree to which it may pass laws that conflict with national laws or jurisprudence. Local laws or edicts come into conflict with the national separation of powers.

The chapters also show significant divergences in the paths taken by different provinces, as decentralization allows and even encourages claims to regional identity. Aceh and South Sulawesi provide an instructive contrast. Briefly, the *relative* religious unity of Aceh has meant that traditionalist *teungku daya*, religious teachers based in (usually rural) Islamic schools, enjoy a great deal of power. Conflicts about who gets to speak in the name of Islam and which textual interpretations should be followed are strongly shaped by Acehnese tensions with Jakarta. These tensions grew out of the efforts to construct the nationwide *Compilation of Islamic Law* and the rejection of some of the *Compilation*'s articles by local teachers who follow the Shafi'i legal school. But they draw their energy from a wider provincial hostility to Jakarta, a hostility that has deep colonial and more immediate postcolonial roots.

By contrast, South Sulawesi has deeply divergent Islamic currents and therefore no one powerful traditionalist body. These divisions leave more room for local tensions and contradictions to emerge in the legal processes than is the case in Aceh, as examples from this volume about the determination of marriage payments and inheritance shares show. The strong role played by cultural notions of shame link village processes of property allocation to the structuring features of social rank and ethnic identity, and sometimes emerge in the courtroom as well.

These national and regional changes provide the background to the specific contributions of this volume's chapters. Taken together, and spanning regions of Indonesia, the chapters speak to three general concerns. First, they underscore the continued importance of starting from local systems of meaning, norms, and power. This is, of course, the starting point for anthropological accounts of legal processes everywhere. In the cases discussed by Atun Wardatun and Rosmah Tami, local ideas and practices of, respectively, shame and reciprocity both facilitate and limit what women do. They are good examples of what Michel Foucault called a '*dispositif*', a set of ideas and mechanisms that are external to the individual but that also shape the individual's orientation to the world.[1]

Three of the chapters show the analytical payoff of focusing on the matter of marriage payments.[2] Studying contemporary Bugis Makassarese society, Tami shows how local dimensions of culture and society shape women's access to property in two ways: in constituting the local social field of property rights and in shaping the reasoning of judges and other officials. The ideas and mechanisms of *siri* – shame, honour, and modesty – both encourage and discourage women from accessing their property rights. She presents the case of *sompa*, a payment from the groom that corresponds to and indexes the bride's status, but, strikingly, may remain unknown to the bride. It may consist of land, money, or other valuables, and if a couple divorce and there are children, it goes to the children. In the case of Becce and Baso, a house was publically stated at the time of the marriage to be *sompa*, but when the marriage collapsed the groom's family protested that the house was really only for show, to uphold *siri*, that it was not intended as *sompa*. In this society, the pronouncement of the *sompa* at the wedding has performative value: it establishes that the bride has a particular status in the eyes of the groom's family. The performative value does not depend on the existence of the object of the pronouncement or any act of material transfer of control. The value does however depend on the belief by wedding guests and family members that it has been given. In this case, protecting the family's *siri* (and the stakes were raised because the child may have been conceived before the marriage) kept Becce from complaining about the failure to receive the *sompa* for her daughter.

One of the key Islamic legal categories involved and invoked in divorce payment disputes is the marriage gift from the husband to the wife, the *mahr*. But as Wardatun, working in Bima, demonstrates, locally *mahr* is embedded in a wider field of marriage payments, and it is the bride's family that provides the marriage payment, the *co'i*. She finds that the social meaning of the payment is

---

1   The term is variously translated as 'mechanism' or 'apparatus'; a good example is in his study of sexuality, see Foucault, 1980.

2   Marriage payments have long been a productive domain for anthropological analysis; see for example Comaroff, 1980.

as a mutually shared institution based on reciprocity (*kacampo fu'u*, literally joint property). Here, the Islamic gift is subsumed in a larger and wider set of exchange-related practices and obligations. As she explains (and the case is similar to that of the Bugis marriage payments), the expected contributions from the husband and wife (or the parents of one or the other) are sensitive to the economic and social status of each. This open-textured nature of norms is based on the key cultural idea that marriage payments are a joint social fact, with both sides contributing. But these understandings leave any later legal determination of *mahr* wide open to competing interpretations, with any particular payment interpreted as *mahr* or not.

Arskal Salim focuses on marriage payments in a comparative analysis of Aceh and South Sulawesi. He points to differing local ideas about what counts as *mahr* and what is another kind of payment. The importance of this analysis is two-fold. First, he shows how and what may be taken to be a straightforward application of Islamic law in fact indexes culturally specific notions of status, honour, and value more generally. Second, he asks how these cross-regional variations shape what happens when disputes arise and are taken either to village-level institutions or to the Islamic courts.

In both provinces, judges look for ways to determine what counts as *mahr* and what does not in the face of conflicting testimonies and unclear memories. In one Aceh case the judges were able to rely on a local requirement that the imam signing the wedding certificate attest to the amount of *mahr*. When judges in these and other provinces stipulate that such evidence is required for a payment to count, they can avoid weighing the plausibility of claims about verbal side-agreements. But our fieldwork evidence from a South Sulawesi village, reported by Salim, shows the weakness in this solution. The village imam certifies as *mahr* those payments that he sees as clearly a marriage gift from husband to wife. But he also acknowledges that local custom specifies that these *sunrang* payments do not become the property of the wife, as Islamic law dictates is the case with *mahr*, but should be returned in case of divorce. If a divorcing wife were to demand to keep such property, she would win a lawsuit because of the written evidence. Here the clear intent of the parties (payments are returned) conflicts with the logic of written evidence (*mahr* is hers to keep). The system is only stable as long as divorcing women seek to avoid the social costs in terms of *siri* by not demanding to retain the *sunrang*.

Second, the chapters highlight women's visions and strategies. These visions and strategies are apparent in some of the chapters just discussed, but others make these issues their focus. Nanda Amalia, for example, looks at inheritance distributions across northern Aceh. She emphasizes the importance of legal reasoning based on the principle of gender equality in Indonesian Supreme

Court decisions. She then asks how local Islamic court judges have decided cases, and looks at the roles played by lawyers and mediators as well as judges. This is an important move, to broaden the field of actors studied. She highlights the role of the Bungong Jeumpa Foundation in mediating inheritance cases, but bases her analysis on a series of detailed ethnographic case studies that allow her to evaluate the increasingly prominent role of lawyers in cases regarding property pursued at Islamic courts. Her conclusion? Lawyers are needed; they tend to be sympathetic to women (and in that regard, are like judges); increasingly they put profits first.

Tutik Hamidah takes a major, and sensitive, high court decision and examines the positions of Muslim women leaders, showing the creative ways that they justify their appraisals of the decision by drawing from science and religion. In 2012, the Indonesian Constitutional Court held that children born out of wedlock have a civil law relationship with their father and with his family, which covers family and property relationships in the form of maintenance and inheritance. The decision covered the children of marriages that followed Islamic rules but were not registered with the state and adulterous unions.

She spoke with women leaders of two major Islamic organizations about the decision. All agreed with the court's decision concerning unregistered (*siri*) marriages, but disagreed among themselves regarding the case of adultery. Some followed a fatwa of the Majelis Ulama Indonesia (Indonesian Scholars' Asssembly, MUI) that in adultery cases the biological father must provide for the child's maintenance and that the child should receive a portion of the father's estate, not through the logic of inheritance law but as an 'obligatory bequest' (*wasiyat wajibah*). One scholar argued that the refusal to grant full inheritance and status rights to children of adulterous fathers was only due to the unavailability of DNA testing when the Islamic legal traditions were developed. Now that the identity of the father can be determined with certainty there is no reason to continue the asymmetry of rights recognition between mother and father. In other words, the birth of the child has Islamic-legal effects, regardless of the marital status of the parents.

Third, contributors document the creative interpretations made by Islamic court judges in order to reach what the judges see as morally appropriate and legally defensible conclusions. Tami's exploration of the case of Nana shows the ingenuity of Indonesian Islamic court judges in using the law to reach what they find to be ethically desirable ends. Nana, a third wife, was blocked from receiving any portion of her deceased husband's property because the marriage was legally flawed (he had claimed to be single while still married to his second wife). But the judge drew on the Islamic mechanism of 'obligatory bequest' to award Nana one-half of what she would have received as his widow. This use is

EPILOGUE 151

interesting in that the obligatory bequest was itself borrowed by the Indonesian creators of the 1991 *Compilation* in order to plug a loophole in Islamic inheritance law. In standard fiqh, when a person dies before his or her parents, that person's children receive nothing because the link has been broken. The problem of the grandchild was solved in Egypt through the obligatory bequest mechanism, and Indonesian judges borrowed it. It is part of the *Compilation*, thus holds legal force. But in this case, it was repurposed to solve another problem, one that had nothing to do with the breaking of the link, but with the disjunction between an ethical obligation and the letter of the law. The judge motivated her decision by mentioning the wife's support of her deceased husband and the judge's sympathy for her plight. The judges also apparently took into consideration that Nana's marriage was valid under prevailing understandings of fiqh, even if in violation of Indonesian positive law.

Still more interesting was the appellate court's response to the appeal made of this judgment. They voided the lower court's ruling, on the (predictable) grounds that Nana's marriage had no legal basis, but they awarded her the house where they had lived and his motorcycle, as *mut'ah*, the gift due the wife upon divorce. Those judges may have had motivations similar to those of the lower court judge, but they apparently found the *mut'ah* category to be less of a flagrant departure from established practices than that of the obligatory bequest.

But judicial discretion and creativity do not always ensure that women receive their rightful property. Two chapters focus on factors that lead judges to award some women lower amounts. Working in distinct regions, the researchers arrive at similar findings in this regard. Euis Nurlaelawati observed West Java courts near Jakarta, and Abidin Nurdin studied courts near Banda Aceh. Each researcher finds that in seeking to arrive at feasible solutions, judges take into account the man's economic capacity and that this may lead them to award a woman less than they otherwise would. They also argue that Indonesia's Islamic courts do not have clear ways to ensure that long-term payments, such as those for child maintenance, are made. Most other payments are payable at the moment of divorce, and the courts can execute these because they have the right to refuse to grant the husband the right to pronounce the divorce unless he pays up in cash. But they do not have a separate police power to enforce child maintenance payments.

Both researchers also point to a problem not with enforcement but with the substance of the laws as they are written, namely that judges may, and sometimes do, deny a wife a payment or lower its level on grounds that she has been 'disobedient'. Here contributors found a great deal of variation in how judges used this article of the Islamic code. Nurlaelawati finds instances when a wife admitted leaving the house without her husband's permission and was considered disobedient. But our studies in Aceh found judges reticent to cite the grounds of disobedience, precisely because it was assumed that in most divorce cases both parties were likely to be neglecting their marital and household obligations. Clearly more empirical work is needed on this issue.

Studies from other Muslim societies also find that some judges interpret the legal framework in such a way as to favour women when possible, for example by using wide definitions of 'harm' (*darar*) done to a woman and narrow definitions of 'disobedience' (*nusyûz*), which is the basis of counterclaims sometimes made by husbands. Courts may favour women to the extent that they see them as the weaker party, sometimes by way of placing the burden of proof on the husband. Such is often the case with regard to husbands' claims of disobedience, as discussed above, for example, or, in a related move, by stipulating, either explicitly or implicitly, that the very fact that the wife brought a divorce suit is prima facia evidence of marital discord and thus grounds for divorce. For example, Tunisian judges take a wife's suit for maintenance as evidence of a husband's failing; it is then up to him to prove that he does pay. They also require the husband to prove claims of disobedience and to show that there was no justification for her disobedience, for example, that leaving the home was not in order to work or to visit relatives (Vincent-Grosso, 2012).

More broadly, a growing number of studies from other Muslim countries have begun to look at the effects of recent legal reforms aiming to bring greater equality to women's and men's experiences and results in Islamic courts. One recent survey of such studies found that women usually win their divorce suits if they pursue the case. In some countries, a major reason for this is the gradual acceptance of marital discord as grounds for dissolution. In Morocco, legal reforms passed in 2004 led to a sharp rise in divorce suits, most brought by, and won by, women, and almost all women who brought suit on grounds of discord, notably easy to prove, won. In other countries recent studies suggest that women's suits based on the husband's absence or failure to adequately support his wife also were granted most of the time.[3]

In our volume, the contributors bring together very different cases from different regions, read through different disciplinary lenses. They converge on the finding that Indonesian Islamic courts have on balance improved the access of women to wealth in divorce and inheritance disputes, and that judges have

---

3 For an overall analysis see Rosen, 2018.

fairly applied the law. In this they agree with the recent findings of other researchers who are working elsewhere. But these findings and these gains, are early and tentative.

Bibliography

Comaroff, J.L. (Ed). (1980). *The meaning of marriage payments*. New York, NY: Academic Press.

Foucault, M. (1980). *The history of sexuality*, Volume I: *An introduction* (R. Hurley, Trans.). New York, NY: Vintage.

Rosen, L. (2018) *Islam and the rule of justice*. Chicago: University of Chicago Press.

Vincent-Grosso, S. (2012). Maktub: An ethnography of evidence in a Tunisian divorce court. In M. Voorhoeve (Ed.), *Family law in Islam* (pp. 171–198). London, England: I.B. Tauris.

Glossary

Adat (Ind.)   Customary law

Aisyiyah (Ind.)   Muhammadiyah-related Muslim organization for women

Akad nikah (Ind.)   Marriage solemnisation

Akte nikah (Ind.)   Marriage certificate

Ampa co'i ndai (Bima)   Bride-paid marriage payment

Arisan (Ind.)   Monthly social savings group with revolving payouts

Aulad (Ar.)   Children (including girls)

Ba'da dukhul (Ar.)   Post consummation of marriage

Bain (Ar.)   Irrevocable divorce

Cerai gugat (Ind.)   Judicial divorce (following the wife's legal action for divorce)

Co'i di pehe (Bima)   Stated payment

Co'i di wa'a (Bima)   Brought wealth, personal property

Cua bantu (Bima)   Reciprocity

Cuu kana'c ngara (Bima)   Status

Da'wah (Ar.) *Dakwah* (Ind.)   Islamic preaching

Dana siwe (Bima)   Female land

Doi balanca (Bugis Mak.)   Wedding expenses payment

Doi menre (Bugis)   Wedding expenses payment

Erang-erang (Bugis Mak.)   Female ornaments

Fatwa (Ar. Ind.)   Legal opinion given by a scholar or group of scholars of Islam

Fiqh (Ar.) Fikih (Ind.)   Islamic jurisprudence

Ghairu muakkadah (Ar.)   Not strongly recommended

Gihaz (Ar.)   House and furniture

Gotong royong (Ind.)   Communal cooperation

Hadd/hudud (Ar.)   Predetermined, fixed punishment

Hadlanah (Ar.)   Right of custody of the children

Hareuta peunulang (Aceh)   Bequest of non-movable property (such as house or land) by parents to daughter upon marriage

Harga diri (Ind.)   Self-esteem

Harta bawaan (Ind.)   Brought wealth, personal property

Hijab (Ar. Ind.)   To cover

Hudud (Ar. Ind.)   *Hadd* offences/fixed penalties in Islamic law

Iddah (Ar. Ind.)   Legally prescribed waiting period during which a woman may not remarry after having been widowed or divorced

Imam (Ar.)   Religious official or leader

Ijab qabul (Ar.) *Ijab kabul* (Ind.)   Marriage contract

Ijtihad (Ar.)   Legal reasoning

Jallo (Bugis. Mak)   To run amuck

Kacampo fu'u (Bima)   Joint property

Kadeni ma do'o (Bima)   Closing or nearing the distance

Karawi kakese (Bima)   Self-funded marriage

Kasasi (Ind.)   Appeal

Kati (Ind.)   Unit of weight equivalent to 625 gr

Kawin sembunyi-sembunyi (Ind.)   To be secretly married

Kebanggaan (Ind.)   Pride

Kehormatan (Ind.)   Honour

Kepala desa (Ind.)   Village chief

Khuluk (Ind.) *khulu'* (Ar.)   A form of Islamic divorce initiated by the wife in which she agrees to pay compensation to the former husband, often by repaying the dowry that was initially given to her

Kiswah (Ar.)   Clothing settlement

Kyai (Ind.)   Muslim leader/jurist

Lise kawing (Bugis)   Lit. wedding substance, small payment

Mahr (Ar.) *Mahar* (Ind.)   Dowry

Mahkamah Konstitusi (Ind.)   Constitutional court

Mahkamah Syar'iyyah (Ind.)   Shari'a court

Mappakasiri (Bugis Mak.)   Causer of humiliation

Martabat (Ind.)   Dignity

Maskan (Ar.)   Accommodation

Mayam (Aceh)   3.3 grams of gold

Mazhab (Ar. Ind.)   School of thought concerning the interpretation of Islamic law. The four Sunni schools are: Hambali, Hanafi, Maliki, and Shafi'i (Syafi'i)

Mo loa nenti nggala ro oka (Bima)   Skillful in farming (literally capable of wielding farming tools)

Muakkadah (Ar.)   Strongly recommended

Muballigh/ah (Ar.)   Male/female Muslim preacher

Muhammadiyah   Reformist/modernist Muslim mass organization

Munas alim ulama NU (Ind.)   NU National Council of Learned Scholars

Muslimat NU (Ind.)   NU-related organization for married women

Muth'ah (Ar.) *Mut'ah* (Ind.)   Compensation fee/gift of consolation

Mut'ah (Ar. Ind.)   Contracted marriage for certain particular period

Nafkah (Ar. Ind.)   Maintenance, economic support

Nafkah iddah (Ar. Ind.)   Post-divorce waiting period maintenance payment

Nafkah mut'ah (Ar. Ind.)   Post-divorce gift payment

Nanre api (Bugis)   Lit. burnt by fire, i.e. all money spent

Ngge'e nuru (Bima)   In-house screening

Nikah mut'ah (Ind.)   Temporary marriage

Nusyuz (Ar.)   Disobedience on part of wife

Nyai (Ind.)   Wife or daughter of a *kyai*

Pabbere' (Bugis)   Wedding gifts

Pesantren (Ind.)   Islamic boarding school

Perempuan (Ind.)   Woman

Pesse (Bugis)   Empathy, feeling of responsibility, care for humiliated person

Peunulang (Aceh)   See *hareuta peunulang*

Piti ka'a (Bima)   Spending money

Qabla al-dhukhul (Ar.)   Prior to consummation of marriage

Qanun (Ar. Ind.)   Islamic laws and regulations enacted by the government

Ripakasiri (Bugis Mak.)   Humiliation/ed

Shabkha (Ar.)   Bridal jewellery

Shari'a (Ar.) *Syariah* (Ind.)   Divine

GLOSSARY

guidance as outlined in the Quran and the Prophetic tradition or Sunna that includes almost all aspects of Islamic belief and practices. It is often (mis)understood to only indicate legal matters.

Silariang (Bugis Mak.)   Elopement

(*nikah*) *siri* (Ar. Ind.)   Unregistered marriage

Siri (Bugis)   Shame, closely related to self-esteem and respect

Sirri (Ar.)   Hidden, secret

Sompa (Bugis)   Payment to bride to express rank

Sunnah muakkadah (Ar.)   Confirmed words and acts of Muhammad that Muslims are strongly encouraged to follow

Sunrang (Makas.)   Payment to bride to express rank

Surat Keputusan (Ind.)   Official decree

Su'udzon (Ar.)   To think ill of someone

Syiqaq (Ar.)   Inharmonious

Talaq (Ar.) Talak (Ind.)   Unilateral divorce under husband's petition

Talaq bain (Ar.)   Irrevocable divorce

Talaq roj'i (Ar.)   Revocable divorce

Tazir (Ar.)   Punishment, unspecified by the Qur'an or hadith

Tarbiyah (Ar. Ind.)   Education

Tuan guru (Sasak)   Religious leader

Uma mone (Bima)   Male house

Ushul fiqh (Ar.)   Islamic legal theory, principles of jurisprudence

Walad (Ar.)   Son

Wali (Ar. Ind.)   Guardian

Wasiah wajibah (Ar.)   Obligatory bequest

Zakat (Ar. Ind.)   Alms tax

Index

Page numbers in **bold** refer to information in tables.

Acehnese communities
  inheritance disputes
    lawyer-client interaction 74–82
    mediation 69, 73, 74–79, 83
    women's status 71–72
  mahr 128–129
    claiming unpaid payments 133–138
    disputes 132–133
  post-divorce payments 123–124
    case studies 113–119
    gifts of consolation 111
    government regulations v Islamic law
      120–122
    iddah maintenance 111
    implementation and enforcement of
      decisions 122–123
    judicial discretion 119
  women's property ownership 109–111
adat law, *see* customary law
adultery
  children born of adultery 61–64
    children born of *siri* marriages com-
      pared 57–60
    rights of children born of adultery
      64–65
  gender differences in attitude 24
ampa co'i ndai (bride-paid marriage payments)
  compensation for lowly status, as 20
  family prestige and 26–27
  government employees 20
  inequality of social status 23–24
  mahr, distinguished from 22
  mutual contribution 22–23
  raising bride's social status 23–24, 25–
    26
  roles of bride and groom 21
  tool of control, as a 24–25
  see also mahr
Aisyiyah (Islamic women's organization)
  56–57
  children born of adultery 61–64
  children born of *siri* marriages 57–60,
    64

appeals
  claims for child support 36–37
  gifts of consolation 36–37
  iddah maintenance 97
  inheritance disputes 74, 74n4, 74n5, 76,
    77
  non-returnable marriage payments
    140–142

bilateral kinship system 102
Bimanese communities
  ampa co'i ndai, see ampa co'i ndai
  compensation, marriage payments as
    20
  government employees 20–21
  groom-testing traditions 21
  mahr/co'i 17–19
  negotiating *mahr* 19–20, 21–23
  principles and practice of *mahr* 15–17
  mahr with personal property and *Surat
    Keputusan* 19–20
Bugis Makassarese communities 8, 30n1
  siri concept 31–32
    case studies 40–41
    inheritance and *siri* 37–39
    social identity and *siri* 41–43
    social location of families 32–33
    sompa compared 34–37
  see also siri; South Sulawesi communities

Catholicism
  divorce 112n6
children born of adultery 61–64
  children born of *siri* marriages compared
    57–60
  rights of children born of adultery 64–
    65
children born of *siri* marriages 57–60
children born out of wedlock
  children born of adultery 61–64
    children born of *siri* marriages com-
      pared 57–60
    rights of children born of adultery
      64–65

INDEX

Constitutional Court Judgment No.
46/PUU-VIII/2010 52, 64–65
controversy 47–48, 53–54
Fatwa No. 11/2012 53–54
law reform 47, 54–55, 56
legal status 47
right to inherit property 7, 54–55
centralization of judiciary 3
New Order Indonesia 4–5
child support 90, 92
appeals 36–37
bilateral kinship system, impact of 102
custody issues 100
lack of enforcement 101–102
reliance on extended family 102
colonialization 3, 112
Compilation of Islamic Law in Indonesia
(Presidential Instruction No.1 1991) 4,
48–49, 49n5, 147
dissolution of marriages 93–94
marriage payments 17, 144
marriage reforms 90, 93
post-divorce rights 90, 93, 103, 109
sanctioning of non-registered marriages
48–49
Constitution 1945 52, 52n14, 74
Constitutional Court Judgment No. 46/PUU-
VIII/2010 52, 64–65
background 51
children born of adultery 61–64
children born of *siri* marriages 57–60
controversy 47–48, 53–54
Muslim/civil law conflict 51–52
registration and legitimacy of marriages
52
status of children born out of wedlock
52–53
women's rights organizations, responses
of 55–57
children born of adultery 61–64
children born of *siri* marriages 57–
60
customary law
codification 1, 3–4
customary marriage payments 132, 144
obligation to return wedding expenses
payment 140–141
see also sompa
inheritance rights 69–70, 72, 79

mediation 79, 83
no entitlement to inheritance 71–72
living *adat* 4
mediation 79, 83
women's property ownership
adat and *shari'a* law compared 109–
111

decentralization, political and cultural 3, 5,
146–147
disobedience as grounds for divorce 8
loss of rights 93, 102–103, 108
dispute settlement
extra-judicial dispute settlement 3
judicial interpretation 2–3
marriage payments disputes 8, 131–133
non-returnable marriage payments
139–142
returnable marriage payments 142–
144
returning marriage payments 138–
139
mediation 69, 73, 74–79, 83
see also inheritance disputes; mediation
divorce
disobedience as grounds for divorce
loss of rights 102–103
government employees **114**
gender difference 24
husband-filed divorces 90, 92
judicial discretion 96–100
monetary awards to women 2
non-tenured workers **118**
post-divorce payments to women 7–8
wife-filed divorces 90, 92
lack of maintenance payments 103

enforcement of family law 122–123, 151–152
child support 101–102, 151
iddah maintenance 104
interpretation and enforcement 146
mut'ah 104
extra-judicial dispute settlement, *see* mediation
extra-marital affairs, *see* adultery

gender-neutral inheritance 71
gifts of consolation 90, 91, 92–94
procedural reform 94–96

160 INDEX

government employees
   ampa co'i ndai 20
   co'i providers 18–19, 23
   iddah maintenance 113
   mut'ah 113
   status and good character 20–21
groom-testing traditions 21

honor, *see siri*

iddah maintenance 90, 91, 92
   confusion surrounding terminology 93
   husband-filed divorces 92
   procedural reform 94–96
   wife-filed divorces 92
illegitimate children, *see* children born out of
   wedlock
independence 3–4
   sompa, impact on 130
Indonesian Commission for Child Protection
   47, 54
inheritance disputes
   case studies 73–82
   legal representatives, relationship with
      74–77
   mediation 69, 73, 74–79, 83
   property disputes 73
      first and second spouses 79–82
      sole daughter and her uncle 77–79
      spouse and step-children, between
         74–77
inheritance dispute resolution (Law No. 7
   1989) 4
inheritance rights
   children born out of wedlock 7
   civil and Islamic law compared 7
   customary rights 72
   gender-neutral inheritance 71–72
   judicial sensitivity to women's rights
      72–73
   legal representation 7
   principle of equal status to male and
      female children 72
   role of lawyers 69–70
   siri 37–40
   women's legal status 69, 70–71
interpretation of Islamic law 1, 4, 27–28,
   146–147
   child support requirements 102

children born out of wedlock 54–55, 64
   inherited property 71, 77–79, 150
   mahr and *sompa* 132–133, 149
Islamic law
   étatisation of Islamic law 4–5, 146–147
   inheritance rights
      civil law compared 7
   judicial interpretation 2–3, 5
   post-divorce payments 120–122
   post-divorce property rights
      dowry awarded at wedding 92
      financial support throughout wedding
         92
      gifts of consolation 92
      share of inheritance on husband's
         death 92
   see also Compilation of Islamic Law in
      Indonesia (Presidential Instruction
      No.1 1991); interpretation of Islamic
      law

joint property
   mahr 17
   legal representation in joint property dis-
      putes 73
      case studies 74–77
judges
   bias 5
   interpretation of Islamic law 2–3, 5
   post-divorce payments 7–8
   training
      equality of inheritance 72–73
judicial discretion 151
   post-divorce rights
      case studies 96–100, 113–120

kacampo fu'u, see mutual contribution

lawyers, *see* legal representation
legal pluralism 1–2
   implications for marriage registration
      48–49
   inheritance disputes 69–70, 71
   marriage legitimacy 49
legal representation
   case studies 74–82
   joint property disputes 74–79
   lack of commitment to parties 80–81
   motivation 82

INDEX

legitimacy of marriages
    case study   51–55
    registration of marriages   48–50
    siri marriages   50n7, 58–60
    status of illegitimate children   48–50
    whether *mahr* required   127–128
Lembaga Bantuan Hukum Asosiasi Perempuan Untuk Keadilan, *see* Women's Association for Justice and Legal Aid
local cultural codes   1
    judicial interpretation   5
    marriage gifts   6
    see also customary law; *mahr; siri*

mahr   2, 6, 15, 127–128
    comparative law   149
    mahr principles   15–16
    negotiation
        compensation, payments as   20
        family prestige   26–27
        government employees   20–21
        mutual contributions   19
        roles of bride and groom   21–27
        women's power   24–25
        women's status   23–24, 25–26
    principles and practice compared   15–17, 27–28
    reciprocity principle   17
    regional perceptions of   127–131
    social status and   16, 128
    see also ampa co'i ndai
marriage payments
    claiming unpaid payments   133–138
    disputes   131–133
    non-returnable marriage payments   139–142
    returnable marriage payments   142–144
    returning marriage payments   138–139
    see also ampa co'i ndai; mahr; sompa
Marriage Law No. 1/1974   4
    children born out of wedlock
        inheritance rights   7, 47, 56
    judicial review of   51–55
    marriage legitimacy   4, 48–50, 51n13
    post-divorce rights   90, 93
        Aceh   111–112
marriage registration
    Marriage Law No. 1/1974   48–49

requirement to legitimize marriages   48–50
mediation
    inheritance disputes   69, 73, 74–80, 83
    unpaid marriage payments   133
Muslimat NU (Islamic women's organization)   56–57
    children born of adultery   61–64
    children born of *siri* marriages   57–60
mut'ah, see gifts of consolation
mut'ah marriages   54n22
mutual contribution   19, 23, 28
    see also ampa co'i ndai

nashiz, see disobedience as grounds for divorce
National Commission on Violence Against Women   47, 54
negotiation of marriage gifts
    ampa co'i ndai   20
    co'i di wa'a/Surat Keputusan and   19–20
    mahr
        compensation, payments as   20
        government employees   20
        mutual contributions   19
New Order Indonesia
    centralization   4
    étatisation of Islamic law   4–5, 146–147

obligatory bequests   39, 150–151
    children born out of wedlock   54, 56, 62–63, 64–65, 150

polygamy   90–91
    absence of *sompa*   38
    inheritance rights of women   58–60, 64, 73, 82
    siri marriages   58–60, 64, 76n11
post-divorce payments   7–8, 123–124
    case studies   113–119
    disputing marriage payments   127
    government regulations v Islamic law   120–122
    implementation and enforcement of decisions   122–123
    judicial discretion   119
    wife-filed divorces   103
    see also post-divorce rights of women

162 INDEX

post-divorce rights of women 7–8, 89–90,
  104–105
  case studies 113–119
  child support 90, 92
    see also child support
  custody of children 90, 92, 100
  gift of consolation 90, 91, 92, 123–124
  government regulations v Islamic law
    120–122
  husband-filed divorces 90
  iddah maintenance 90, 91, 92, 104, 123–
    124
    see also iddah maintenance
  implementation and enforcement of
    decisions 122–123
  Islamic law post-divorce property rights
    dowry awarded at wedding 92
    financial support throughout wedding
      92
    gifts of consolation 92
    share of inheritance on husband's
      death 92
  judicial discretion 119
  Marriage Law (Law No. 1 1974) 90
  research studies 107–109
  wife-filed divorces 90
Protestantism
  divorce 112

reciprocity principle
  mahr 17
regional differences 147
  marriage payments 148–149
registration of marriages, *see* marriage registration

shari'a law, *see* Islamic law
siri 6–7, 43
  access to property 42–43
  Bugis Makassarese communities 30
    diginity and humanity 31
    divorce 35–37
    inheritance 37–40
    interpersonal relationships and shared
      responsibility 31–32
    reaction when *siri* offended 31
    sompa 34–37

children born of *siri* marriages 57–60
divorce 35–37, 51n10
meaning of *siri* 6, 31
siri marriages 50, 50n7
sompa 34–35
  divorce 35–37
  inheritance 37–40
social identities, relationship with 41–
  42
see also sompa
social status of women
  ampa co'i ndai 23–24, 25–26
  government employees 20–21
  mahr 16, 23–24, 25–26
  misrepresentation of wedding expenses
    33n2
sompa
  access to property 42–43
  children and 36
  divorce 35–37
  inheritance 37–40
  negotiation 35
  siri and Bugis Makassarese communities
    34–35
    case studies 35–37
  status, importance of 33, 36–37
  value of gifts 32–33
South Sulawesi communities
  doi menre 129–130
  mahr 129–131
    disputes 131–132
  sompa 37, 129–131, 132
  siri 43, 129–131
  wasiah wajibah 39
  see also Bugis Makassarese communities
Surat Keputusan, see government employees
sunrang, see sompa

wasiah wajibah, see obligatory bequests
Women's Association for Justice and Legal
  Aid 40–41
women's rights organizations
  Aisyiyah 56–57
  Muslimat NU 56–57
  Women's Association for Justice and Legal
    Aid 40–41

Printed in the United States
By Bookmasters